"SMALL TOWN ENTERTAINMENT" PRESENTS

A

(((COOTER BROWN PRODUCTION)))

BROTHERLY LOVE

A NOVEL

BY

WILL J. SIMS

ISBN: 1-58721-683-3

Copyedited by Susan Christophersen

1st Books rev.-6/23/00

ABOUT THE BOOK

Brotherly Love is the ***Emmy winning*** story of Will Taylor's escape from the barriers of a small Mississippi town, in order to achieve his dream of becoming an Air Traffic Controller in the Federal Aviation Administration. It is the story of Will and James, brothers whose lives take distinctly opposite paths. Will's life is falling apart. He tries to please his mother, wife, brother, and employer, and ends up pleasing no one.

Brotherly Love is the winner of three Emmy awards; Best Producer/Director, Best Informational Program, and Best Lighting. It also won the Procter and Gamble Dreambuilder Celebration Playwright Competition of 1999. The television movie will air in the Midwest during January/July of 2000, with the theatrical production being presented in the spring of 2000.

Comments about the TV movie:

"The opening scene pretty much dictates the tone of the show. Sims, and his brother, walk by a Confederate statue in Mississippi and James spits on it." *Skip Hess, The Indianapolis Star/News, Indianapolis, Indiana.*

"Brotherly Love, a script written by Will J. Sims of Indianapolis, is the story of Will and James, brothers whose lives take opposite paths. It spans 30 years in the life of a man who must make difficult choices when brotherly love stands in the way of his dreams." *Herald-Leader Staff, The Lexington Herald-Leader, Lexington, Kentucky.*

"Jim Friedman, one of the city's most oft-awarded filmmakers with 42 Emmys and a housefull of other awards, is gearing up for the production of Brotherly Love. The outstanding script, written by Will J. Sims of Indianapolis, is about two brothers whose lives take different paths - one self-destructive, one successful." *Jim Knippenberg, The Cincinnati Enquirer, Cincinnati, Ohio.*

BOOK DEDICATION

This book is dedicated to my mother, Mrs. Sallie A. Sims, the sweetest person in the world. Your many years of struggles have not been in vain.

This book is also dedicated to my loving wife and partner, Lisa M. Montgomery, thanks for being there babe; and our two marvelous children, Kristin and Corey; to my father, Mr. James Sims, Sr.; to my in-laws, Mrs. Carol and Mr. Ronald Montgomery, Lori, and Heather; to my sisters, Laura, Ada, and Nora (and Henry, her husband); to my Great Aunt Marie Sims – thanks for opening up your home to all the kids in the neighborhood; and lastly, but definitely not least, my brother James – Much Love…One Day At A Time.

INTRODUCTION

Air Traffic Control is without a doubt, one of the most challenging occupations in today's society. An Air Traffic Control Specialist is described often as one who provides for the safe, orderly, and expeditious flow of air traffic; both in the air and on the ground. The definition may sound simple, but the job is a highly complicated one. It requires the ability to think abstractly, establish priorities, and do first things first. It also requires the ability to carry mental pictures and have automatic recall. The job is tough, and millions of human lives depend on a controller's ability to make the right decisions quickly every day.

I have always been fascinated by aviation, as early as elementary school. I spent most of my days as a young boy reading about airplanes and making airplane models. My lifelong dream was to escape the racial barriers of a small Mississippi town, and pursue a career with the Federal Aviation Administration as an Air Traffic Controller.

Although I successfully fulfilled my lifelong dream, it was disappointedly tarnished as a result of dealing with the hostilities that existed in the organization, as well as dealing with my brother's chemical dependency.

"Who in tha' heck is Cooter Brown?"

FADE IN:

EXT—BACKYARD OF RESIDENCE ON LAKE— INDIANAPOLIS, INDIANA

As I sit on the patio with my wife, Lisa, watching our two children fish in the lake, I can't help but wonder how much impact the stress of the previous year's occurrences will have on their lives. We move slowly back and forth as we sit on the bench swing. Lisa sips a glass of lemonade; I lay my head on her lap, and we both marvel at how much Kristin, 11, and Corey, 8, enjoy having a large lake right in their own back yard. The only thing missing is a retriever, and I'm the last holdout on that idea because I know how much responsibility comes with owning a dog.

Corey laughs uncontrollably as he tries to reel in a fish, "Look, Kristin, I got one! What do I do?"

Kristin drops her rod and runs over to Corey, "Reel him in, Corey, just like Dad showed you!"

Corey struggles with the fish and finally reels him in. They both jump up and down with excitement.

Corey turns and says, "Dad, look what I caught! He's a big one!"

Lisa and I pause from our conversation and focus our attention on the kids.

Laughing, I say to Corey, "Way to go, Corey. Is that a fish or a baby shark?"

Kristin, who inherited her quick wit from her mother, is quick to say, "Dad, don't you know that sharks don't live in lakes?"

Of course, Lisa chimes in, "Your father doesn't know any better; he grew up in Mississippi."

We all laugh; I face Lisa, partially raising my sunglasses before I answer, "Thank God I did because the kids never would have learned how to fish, *Miss, I've never been out of the city of St. Louis!*"

Kristin and Corey face each other and Kristin says, "Oh no, Corey, there they go again."

Corey puts an end to our teasing by asking, "Dad, can I call Grandma and Uncle James and tell them about the fish I caught?"

Kristin looks at Corey in amazement. Lisa and I stop talking immediately; I try to neutralize the grief on my face while struggling for an answer.

The only one that comes to mind is, "Not right now, Corey. Maybe we will later."

It seems to temporarily satisfy him and they both resume their fishing.

Corey's question opened an old wound and a tear rolls down my cheek underneath my sunglasses. Lisa brushes the tear away with her finger, saying, "Will, how long are you going to continue to blame yourself for what happened? Hell, it's been three years!"

I decide not to answer her. Lisa sighs, gets up, and walks to the edge of the lake where Kristin and Corey are fishing.

As I lay in the swing, I reminisce about my past life experiences and wonder whether I'd made the right choices.

It's been three long years since I committed the most unspeakable act known to man. An act that resulted in my mother's stroke.

During the last three years, I've managed to avoid seeing my mother's face. I often replay all the years of my life, hoping to find some sort of justification for what I did. Although there are hundreds of rationalizations, none seem to be good enough, and I'm still searching for the nerve to see my mother's face again.

EXT-SMALL TOWN OF BRANDON,
MISSISSIPPI-1972 (FLASHBACK)

My name is Will Taylor and I was born in December of 1963 in the small Bible Belt town of Brandon, Mississippi.

Throughout my childhood, my mother would often say, "Your birth year will forever be remembered in history."

That was the year that the famous civil rights leader Medgar Evers was assassinated in nearby Jackson, Mississippi. The year of 1963 will always reserve a special place in the history of the struggle for equality in America.

The town of Brandon, Mississippi was home for a population of around 2,000 at the time my brother James and I were growing up. It consisted of several Mom-and-Pop stores and businesses, a small jailhouse, and one traffic light in the middle of town. The town was divided by imaginary racial boundaries that separated the blacks living on one side of town from the whites living on the other.

Brandon is a small town located just down the road from Pearl, our fiercest high school rival and the town where the so-called cult member Luke Woodham shot several of his classmates.

Brandon has two claims to fame: as the one-time home of Mary Ann Mobley, actress and former Miss America, 1959; and the town's name was used at the beginning of the movie Platoon.

In the middle of town stands a thirty-seven foot monument of a Confederate soldier with a Confederate flag in one hand and a rifle in the other. The inscription: *Men Die, Principles Live Forever* is engraved at the base. The monument marks the site where, during the Civil War, General Sherman had his Yankee soldiers stack arms while they burned and looted Brandon on their way to Vicksburg. For whatever reason, the people in Brandon seemed to accept the monument as just another part of the town, and its presence was no big deal to most of them. As a kid, though, I wondered why it didn't seem to bother anyone other than my brother James and I. Even today, the monument still stands, serving as a reminder of the troubled past rooted deeply in the red hills of Mississippi.

My parents are very religious and my family attended church every Sunday. My father and mother were married at a young age, and neither had much of an education.

My mother is a strong and caring woman, much like an angel, and would give her last meal to a stranger if the need arose. She made it as far as the tenth grade before her father made her quit school and work in the cotton fields.

My father, on the other hand, had only a third-grade education. His mother believed that work was more important than school. Therefore, when my father turned nine years old, he was made to work in the cotton fields also.

My father was a strict parent. He demanded respect from all the family and didn't hesitate to use his belt to discipline my older brother James and myself. Often, he came home tired and depressed after working long hours at low-paying jobs. He took his stress out on the rest of the family. We had the scars to prove it.

James was three years my elder and we grew up close. I idolized him and wanted to be just like him in every way. Normally, when James received discipline from my father, I did as well because I always followed in his footsteps.

Our house was small with only five rooms; one of which was the bathroom. The family room was modestly decorated with various old furnishings and my father's worn recliner. The walls were wood paneling, and the flooring was nothing more than torn, worn linoleum.

James and I shared a room. Our small bedroom was furnished with a small dresser, tattered curtains, and a portable fan that offered little relief during the hot, humid Mississippi nights. Our few clothes hung in a small closet whose door was missing.

My grandmother, whom we called Big Mama, worked as a nanny for a white family on the other side of town. She often talked -- and most definitely looked -- the part of the nanny from Gone with the Wind. She wore an old dress and apron that came down to her ankles; she tied a red bandanna around her head.

Sometimes Big Mama would take James and me along with her to work. Most of the time, the purpose was for us to try on clothes that had become too small for the white kids of the family who employed her. We never wanted to go with Big Mama to work; we hated the idea of wearing white kids' clothes.

It embarrassed us to see Big Mama saying "Yes, ma'am" and "Yes, sir" to people who were half her age. As kids, James and I made a vow never to say "Yes, ma'am" or "Yes, sir" to anyone, regardless of whom they were. When we didn't say it at the white folks' house, Big Mama would chastise us both and tell our father when we got home. This, of course, would usually lead to a beating from our father.

Growing up in the small town of Brandon also meant dealing with the Ku Klux Klan. The Klan would hold regular meetings and even pass out literature at the one traffic light in town. Sometimes, on the way from school, we had to pass by the Klan members passing out literature. My brother and I, along with our friends, often threw stones at them and made jokes, not realizing how dangerous it could have been. A few of the Klan members gave chase sometimes but never caught any of us.

I remember sneaking into town one Saturday with James. As we walked down the main street past the monument of the Confederate soldier, James decided to spit on it.

Puzzled, I asked, "Wha'd you go and do that for, James?"

"'Cause I hate this town and everything that statue stands for!"

Too young to fully comprehend his answer, I asked, "What are you talkin' bout?"

"Never mind. You'll see when you get older."

My brother and I always went to the same small Mom-and-Pop store. The store owner was white but was always nice to my family. My family seemed to be accepted by the whites in town, probably because my grandmother helped raise most of their kids and because my father was known as a hard-working man who minded his own business.

The elderly store owner said to James, "Ain't ya'll Genora Taylor's grandbabies?

James and I stared at each other.

7

"Well, speak up."

James hesitantly answered, "Yeah, she our grandma."

The store owner grabbed James by the arm. "Don't ya mean 'yes suh,' boy?"

James' stubbornness kicked in and he displayed no fear. James refused to submit. I spoke up out of fear for what the store owner might do.

"Yes, suh, she our grandma," I said nervously, looking down at the floor.

James frowned at me, showing his disapproval of submitting to the store owner's demand.

Forcefully letting go of James' arm, the storeowner said, "Looks like yo' li'l brother has mo' manners than you. I got haf a mind to tell yo' grandma you being disrespectful. I know she'll tan yo' hide."

James answered, "We just want ta buy some ice cream."

"Put yo' money away, boy. I give it to ya for free cuz I know yo' grandma. 'Sides, there's some goin's on in town today so ya'll best be gettin home."

There was a Klan rally on the other side of town, which usually meant that the members would be drinking and getting rowdy. The rallies were a frequent occurrence and most blacks simply ignored them because they seldom ended in violence. It was usually just a reason for a few uneducated whites to get together and have a drinking party in town.

Unfortunately, the rally was over about the time we were on the road home. From behind, we heard the sound of an approaching vehicle. The vehicle drew closer. It was an old pick-up truck with a Confederate flag painted on the hood. Three men in the cab wore Klan attire and they were driving fast. Very fast. The truck swerved and the men threw beer cans out the window.

As the truck approached us, we heard, "Run over the niggers!"

The driver headed for the shoulder of the road where James and I were walking.

James yelled, "Shit! It's some of those drunk-ass crackers from that Klan rally!"

James jumped off the road into the ditch, thinking I was right behind him. I was too terrified to move, refusing to believe the driver would deliberately hit us.

I stood there in shock and tried to brace myself for the impact.

James yelled, "Will, what tha hell you doin? Get out of the way! Come on, Will!"

Just as the truck was about six feet from striking us, James swooped up and grabbed me and threw us both into the ditch. The truck barely missed us and kept going on down the road. We could see the men in the truck laughing.

James pulled me to my feet and tried to dust off our soiled clothes. I looked down to see that I had wet my pants and I began to cry.

James asked, "What's the matta, you hurt?"

"No. Just scared."

"Well, you don't have to be scared; they long gone. Those Klan guys a bunch a' stupid asses anyway. You don't never haf ta be 'fraid a' them. Come on, we gotta get home before Daddy finds out."

We regained our composure and hurried home. James and I entered the house, only to find my father in the family room, sitting in his old recliner. He held a large belt in his hands.

As soon as he saw us, we stopped in our tracks. He stood up. "Where tha hell ya'll been? Ya'll been sneaking inta town again?" His voice was hard and loud.

James answered, "No, suh, we was just down the road with our friends playing."

"Boy, don't lie to me. I can see those ice cream stains all over ya brother's clothes. Will, did ya'll sneak inta town again?"

I looked at James and then down at the floor. Frightened, I said, "We only sneak inta town because you won't take us."

"Boy, I work all damn day. When I suppose to find time to take ya'll lil asses inta town?"

I was terrified, but James always had nerves of steel. My father leaned over until he was about two inches from James' face.

"Why you lie to me, James?"

9

I will never forget James' answer as long as I live. Stubborn as always, he looked my father square in the face without blinking and said, "What's the difference? You gon' whip us anyway!"

INT—TAYLOR HOME—BRANDON, MISSISSIPPI

James and I lay in bed listening to the Jackson State University football game on his small, portable radio. As usual, Sweetness himself, none other than Mr. Walter Payton, was unstoppable. Back then, every kid in the neighborhood pretended to be Payton and tried to imitate his moves.

My mother finally returned home. She entered our bedroom and sadly discovered the welts on our legs and arms from the beating we had received. She placed her hand over her mouth in dismay.

"Mama, where you been?" I asked.

James looked at her and said, "I'm gon' kick his ass when I grow up."

My mother and I laughed at James' comment, but then she said seriously, "James you don't mean that, and you betta stop that cussing."

"Yes I do! I hate him fa' always whippin' us for anything. It seem like he never has anything good to say to us. He always yellin'."

The only excuse my mother could offer was, "I know he's hard on ya, but it's only 'cause he never had a father. He was raised by ya grandma, who was very strict on him."

My mother's answer didn't sit well with James. "Mama, he treats you like dirt. Why you stay with him?"

"I don't know. I guess I always search fa' tha good in people, and yo' father does have some good ways. I just keep praying to tha lord that he'll see fit to change his ways."

My mother noticed our soiled clothes in the corner of the room, "How'd you guys get yo' clothes so dirty?"

"On the way back from town, some Klan guys in a truck almost ran over us. We jumped in a ditch to keep from being run over," I said.

James looked at me with a sarcastic smirk, prompting me to say, "Well, I needed a li'l help from James."

My mother asked, "Did you guys tell yo' father what happened?"

James replied, "We couldn't. He was too busy givin' us a ass-whippin."

My mother kissed James and me on the cheek and pulled the covers up. She walked down the short hall to the family room where my father was sitting in his worn recliner, drinking beer and watching television. James and I could hear their conversation from our bedroom.

My mother asked, "Why you feel ya need to be so hard on these boys? You beat them like they was some runaway slaves."

As usual, my father was uninterested in anything she had to say; "It's fa' they own good. If they break the rules, they be punished."

"They ya sons. If ya don't treat them with respect, then they won't respect you when they grown," she said. "Did they tell ya they almost got run over by some Klan rednecks today?"

My father let out a loud burp before answering, "Good! Maybe it teach they li'l asses to stay home next time."

Scene 4

INT - TAYLOR HOME - KITCHEN

My days in grade school and junior high were spent trying to maintain good grades and trying to fit in with friends who thought being smart was not cool. I wanted to fit in with friends so desperately, I thought that hiding the truth about receiving perfect scores was the way to do it.

In the South of the 1970s, a black student who excelled academically got labeled by most other black students as trying to be white. I was successful with my deception about my grades until I reached high school. By that time, I didn't care what people thought of me because growing up in a household with an abusive father had cheated me of my years of adolescence, and made me a man well before my time.

It also didn't hurt to have a big brother who was a senior, twice my size, and the captain on the football team. The few times that I did have a beef with someone, James seemed to show up at the right time.

My second year of high school proved to be quite different. James had graduated, and he and my father seemed to argue all the time. It finally came to the point where my brother knew that he had to leave home in order to get away from my father's reign. He did this by joining the "army." His first assignment was to an artillery unit at a base in Germany. He wrote me occasionally. James loved Germany but hated his unit.

In his letters, James explained, "Most of the time our unit sleeps outside in tents during the cold, snowy, winter months of Germany. In order to help deal with being outside in the cold, we drink alcohol and smoke dope. My sergeant knows about the alcohol and drugs, but he always look the other way."

My senior year was short but memorable. I'd taken enough classes during my previous three years that I had to attend only one semester of my senior year to graduate. My grade point average for the previous three years was around 3.6, and I was hoping to receive an academic scholarship to a university.

My own differences with my father grew more pronounced, and we also were having a lot of arguments. I was the youngest and I think that bothered him. It was as if he had lost control of his household.

I had been preparing for months to take the college SAT test. On the night before the test, I was studying at the kitchen table. My father came home in one of his, "mad-at-the-world-moods," and started in on my mother.

She had just begun preparing dinner and was on the telephone with a friend. My father entered the kitchen, stared coldly at my mother, and shook his head in disgust. Then he ripped the telephone off the wall.

"What tha hell you been doing? When I come home, I 'spect you to have dinner ready. I been workin my ass off all day and I'm ready fa' a good meal."

For some reason, my mother refused to cower this time. "I been workin all day too and I'm just gettin' home. But now since you want to act a fool, you can cook fa' ya'self."

He hit her across the face.

By then, I was totally fed up with my father and his mood swings. I was also fed up with the mental and physical abuse of my mother. That particular night, I felt that I had reached manhood and decided to challenge my father. I moved quickly from my seat at the kitchen table and came to my mother's rescue.

As he prepared to strike her again, I grabbed my father's arm. "Dad, that's enough. I think you've gotten your point across."

My father turned to me in disbelief. "I'm 'fraid you picked the wrong day to try to be a man!" He grabbed hold and threw me across the kitchen table.

By this time, my mother had made her way to their bedroom.

As I slowly picked myself off the floor, I saw my father approaching me with fury in his eyes. That's when I started to realize that maybe, I *had* chosen the wrong time to prove my manhood. My father grabbed me by the throat and lifted my small, 150-pound frame off the floor, pinning me against the wall.

My mother emerged from the bedroom with my father's 38 pistol and screamed, "IF YOU HIT MY SON AGAIN, SO HELP ME I'LL KILL YOU WHERE YOU STAND! LET HIM GO, RIGHT NOW!"

I had been terrified of my father many times before, but at that moment, I was even more afraid of my mother than I'd ever been of my father. I was just thankful that she was on my side.

My father, however, was not. He did not believe her and moved menacingly toward her.

He called her bluff. "I'll take that pistol and…"

My mother pulled the trigger and fired. The bullet just missed his left shoulder. My father and I both ducked. His jaws tightened as he glared at her; she glared back, refusing to lower the gun and still as the statue of the Confederate soldier holding his post in the middle of town. He wasted no time in storming out of the house without saying a word.

My father never thought my mother would have the nerve to stand up to him -- and certainly with a gun. That moment, I learned that everyone has a breaking point.

My mother knelt to the floor and started to cry. I took the gun away from her and hid it in my room just in case my father returned home later, still acting loony.

I came back to my mother's side and began to comfort her as best as I could. "Are you all right, Mama?"

She tried to reassure me as best she could. "I'll be fine, baby. That's the last time I ever let him put his hands on me. God knows I love him, but he ever hits me again, I'll kill him dead."

"Mama, why have you put up with this treatment all these years?" I asked.

"I guess I keep on tellin' myself that he gon' change."

My mother's religious beliefs dictate that marriage should last forever. To her, with God and prayer, no problem is insurmountable, including a bad marriage.

As I had often done before, I continued to talk with my mother. That particular night, I felt closer to my mother than ever before.

"I was surprised ta see you come ta my rescue. I realize now that you no longa my baby boy, but a young man," she whispered, as she tried to find the strength to smile.

She continued to talk until she fell asleep. I picked her up, carried her to my room, and placed her on my bed.

As I laid her down, she awoke momentarily, "Make Mama a promise?"

"What kinda promise, Mama?"

"Promise me that you'll neva yell at or hit a woman as long as you live."

I smiled, kissed her on the cheek, and said goodnight.

She fell asleep again, and I locked my bedroom door. I sat in my faded old recliner in my room and spent the rest of the morning trying to digest most of the conversation that my mother and I had.

The next thing I remember was my radio alarm going off and waking up very tired. My mother was also awakened by the alarm, and we both knew that we had to get ready for work and school.

Sometime during the early morning, my father had returned to get dressed for work. My mother and I could tell by the aroma of his cheap cologne still lingering in the air and the fact that his work boots were gone. I was glad that he didn't cause a scene when he returned.

Before my mother left for work, she told me how much she enjoyed the talk we had the night before.

She kissed me on the cheek and said, "I'm so proud of you, Will. I know you tired and upset, but I'm still glad you goin' to school today."

I didn't have the nerve to tell my mother that I was taking the college SAT at school that day. She knew how long and hard I had studied to prepare myself, and it would have broken her heart.

I took the test that morning at school, and right away I knew it was a mistake. I was unable to concentrate and caught myself falling asleep several times during the course of the test. When the test was over, I knew I'd probably blown my chance to really do well, and likewise, my chances for an academic scholarship.

Scene 5

EXT—TAYLOR HOME—FRONT LAWN

After graduation, during that summer of 1981, my brother's three-year hitch with the army was over and he returned home. It was a hot Saturday morning and, although I had my shirt off, it provided little relief while mowing the lawn.

My mother wore an old apron and a large straw hat while working in her flowerbed. A car speeding down the gravel road leading to the house caught our attention. I turned off the lawn mower. My mother slowly stood from her kneeling position, and we both stared at the approaching car.

"Lord 'a mercy! Who in tha world is that drivin' like they drunk as Cooter Brown?" my mother said as she broke the silence.

"It's a taxicab, Mama," I answered hesitantly.

"What in tha world is a taxicab doin' in Brandon?" she asked.

The taxicab finally came to a stop in our gravel driveway. The driver exited and opened the back door. James, in his army uniform and sunglasses, stepped out of the taxi. My mother dropped the flowers that she was holding and let out a scream. She charged James with outstretched arms, and he teased her by running around the front lawn in circles as she gave chase.

When my mother grew tired, she stood in one place, placing her hands on her hips, "James, I ain't gonna chase you all over this yard! I ain't seen you in three years since you left fa Germany. You betta come here, boy, and gimme' a hug."

Smiling from ear to ear, James said, "Hey, Mama. How ya doin?" as he embraced her.

My mother began to cry and could barely speak, "I'm doin just fine now that ya home safe."

James walked over to me, slowly taking off his sunglasses, and gave me a hug.

"What's up, li'l brother? I guess you ain't li'l no mo; you bigga than me."

"What's up, Sarge? Welcome home." My greeting brought a mischievous smile to James' face.

17

"I'm happy to say I ain't a Sarge no mo'. Hit my platoon leader and got myself a permanent vacation. Glad to be home and don't want no part of Uncle Sam again."

James walked over to the taxi driver and took out a wad of cash, "Here's yo' money. Think you can find yo' way back to the airport?"

The taxi driver paused momentarily before answering, "Yeah, I think so. There's only one main road in town."

"Just make a right turn at that sorry-ass monument of that Confederate soldier and it'll take you straight to Hwy. 80. The airport be about seven miles down on yo right."

The taxi driver shook hands with James. "I got it, James. Good luck to ya, here."

My mother, James, and I watched as the taxi drove down the gravel road. We entered the house and sat in the family room; it wasn't long before my father arrived home from his job.

He entered the house and was surprised to see James sitting on the sofa, "Well I be damn, look what the cat drug in! When you get home, James?"

James stood before answering, "How ya doin, Daddy?"

My father wasted no time in asking, "You home fa good?"

"Yeah, fa a while."

"What tha hell you plan on doin now? I hope you ain't planning on stayin' here."

My father and James had a brief stare down. James smiled and tried to mask his anger while shaking his head.

"I see some things haven't changed a bit. Don't worry, old man, I don't plan on stayin' under the same roof with you. I gots a li'l money saved up and I'll be gettin' my own place. But I'll be close by, case mama wanna come live with me. I take care of her."

My father was angered by James' answer, but this was one of the few times that he remained speechless. He stormed down the hall to his bedroom, slamming the door loudly behind him.

We continued our conversation until retiring for the night. As James and I lay in bed, we tried to catch up on three years worth of separation. It was a hot, Mississippi night and the small portable fan in the window did little about that.

James told me about all the wild adventures of his military career and I seemed to have a million questions for him.

"James, what are those German women like?"

"They called *frauleins,* and they treat you like a king. They wait on you hand and foot all the time."

My curiosity was piqued. "Man, that sounds great. It sounds like a whole world apart from Brandon."

"Believe me, li'l brother, it is. One day you'll find out there's mo' to life than Brandon has ta offer."

I proceeded to tell him about my academic accomplishments in high school.

"Damn, with those good grades, I know you got a scholarship somewhere, didn't you?" he asked.

"Nope, I blew the SAT test. Old dude came home trippin' the night before, and I stayed up all night with mama."

Concerned, he asked, "Anybody get hurt?"

"Mama got her nose busted, and I got thrown across the kitchen table. He came to his senses when Mama got a hold of his 38."

"Good for her; it's bout time. She shoulda done that a long time ago when he was whippin' our ass."

Scene 6

INT—TAYLOR HOME—KITCHEN

James had managed to save a great deal of money in Germany. Within a week, he had purchased a new car and was living in his own apartment.

That summer, I had a job at a small store in town, and after work, I would spend time at my brother's place. It was cool because I could take girls there, and they were always impressed by my brother's apartment. Most of the time, my brother would be there with one or two girls himself. All the local girls seemed to like him and he acquired a reputation for throwing wild parties. James was a nice dresser and didn't mind spending money on women, which I'm sure didn't hurt his reputation any.

The summer came to an end and I was starting the fall semester at the local community college. I applied for a federal grant, which paid most of my tuition. I was able to pay for the rest with money that I saved while working over the summer.

By the end of the first semester of my freshman year in college, I received 15 credit hours toward a Computer Science degree. Although my interest since childhood had centered on aviation, there were no aviation courses offered at the Community College. So, I adopted Computer Science as a major.

By now, James was having trouble adjusting to life outside the military. He had been fired from several jobs for not showing up for work and for getting caught smoking marijuana.

The tension between my father and I had reached its boiling point. I could no longer stand to be in the same room with him. All his years of working a job that he hated had taken their toll – on him and, therefore, on us.

The last disagreement that I had with my father will always stick out in my mind because it was so trivial.

I was watching television with my mother and father in the family room. I had just started to snack on some potato chips when my father commented, "Will, do you have ta chew dem damned potato chips so loud?"

That particular night, I was not in the mood for any type of argument with my father; it seemed pointless and futile. And for the first time, I felt sorry for him. I understood that his lack of education, as well as the limited opportunities that life had dealt him, had made him a cold, cruel person. I simply stood up and left the room without a word. I'm sure this caught my father by surprise because most of his negative comments normally started shouting matches between us.

It was at that point that I decided I couldn't take any more verbal abuse from my father and was ready to leave that small Mississippi town.

A few days later, I went to see an Air Force recruiter. My goal was to get away from the south and all its prejudices while pursuing a career in aviation. Pilot training was my first choice. Unfortunately, I discovered that I was not eligible. Therefore, I decided on a career in Air Traffic Control. I figured it would be the next best career in aviation.

I completed the enlistment procedures. However, I was reluctant to tell my mother I'd enlisted in the Air Force. My quitting school would break her heart.

When I found out that I'd passed the military examinations, I hesitantly gave my mother the news.

Slowly, I emerged from my bedroom and walked into the kitchen.

My mother was preparing dinner. "Mama, I got somethin' to tell you."

"What is it, baby?"

I took a deep breath. "Mama, I joined the Air Force. I'm leaving next week."

As expected, she did not take the news well. "What you talkin' bout?"

Regretfully, I informed her, "I already signed the papers."

"Well, I don't think so!" she yelled. "You gon' stay right here and finish college. I'm goin' down to that Air Force tomorrow and tear up that paperwork."

My mother was under the impression that she had to concur with the enlistment paperwork, I sadly reminded her, "Mama, I'm eighteen years old and I don't need your consent."

22

It was the hardest thing for me to speak those words to the lady I cared for more than anything in the world.

My mother turned her back to me and continued to prepare dinner. I stood there watching her for a moment before dropping my head in sadness. As I left the kitchen and walked back to my bedroom, I could hear the clanging of pots and pans voicing her disapproval.

My mother did not speak for the rest of that afternoon, until my father arrived. When my father came through the door, he seemed to feel the tension in the house. This was one afternoon that he held his usual irritability in check, at least at first. He could see that my mother was upset and he didn't know the reason. While my mother prepared dinner, she continued to fling pots, pans, and plates almost to the point of breaking them.

My father remained quiet for a time until he finally worked up the nerve to break the silence.

"Don't break them damn dishes; we can't 'fford ta buy new ones."

Hearing this from my room, I thought, "Oh boy, you shouldn't have said that!"

Next came a scream and the crash of shattering glass. I ran out of my room and into the kitchen. Broken glass all over the floor. My father was bleeding from a laceration on the side of his face. My mother had thrown a glass at him, striking her target.

My father looked stunned.

"What tha hell's tha matta wit you?" he finally managed to yell.

My mother angrily replied, "I hope you finally happy, you done made both my sons leave home."

She told him about my enlistment and that I would be leaving soon to get away from him. Then she stormed out of the kitchen and down the hall to her bedroom, slamming the door.

My father turned to look at me. The silence, probably only a moment's worth, seemed to last five minutes. It was as if he was searching for any words that might change the situation. Of course, there weren't any. I just turned and walked away.

Scene 7

INT—JAMES' APARTMENT—FAREWELL PARTY

The weekend before I was scheduled to leave, James decided to throw me a farewell party. His apartment was decorated in late '70's decor and had two modest bedrooms. It was the ultimate bachelor pad, complete with all the latest music.

About fifty people were scattered throughout the apartment, with plenty of alcohol and drugs to go around. I made my way around the apartment greeting my brother's friends and mine while the d. j. blasted the sounds of *Mary Jane*, by Rick James. As the song played, several people fired up joints and began to pass them around.

I found a retreat in the corner, but it was only momentary. James spotted me and came over with drink in hand.

"There you are, li'l brother! I been lookin all over fa' you. I thought you mighta been in tha bedroom gettin' yo' groove on."

I gave James a sarcastic smirk before answering, "Not hardly! Not with any of those skeezers."

He rested his left arm on my shoulder, "Hey, don't talk 'bout my women like that. Sides, this yo' last weekend in town and big brother gon' make sure you have a good time. Come wit me."

James grabbed me by the arm and led me to the middle of the family room. He motioned to the d.j. to cut the music.

"Yo, everybody, listen up. This a farewell party for my baby brother. He leavin' for tha Air Force in a couple days and I want ya'll to make sure he have a good time tonight. Specially ya'll ladies, okay. That's all I have ta say. Ya'll keep on partying."

Everyone began to clap and lift their drinks in a toast. The d.j. started to blast the music again.

I was completely embarrassed by James' speech, "What the hell you do that for, James?"

With typical nonchalance, he laughed before answering, "I'm tryin to get you some fat rabbit before you leave town, boy."

"What the hell is 'fat rabbit'?"

James gave me his patented *you dumb ass* look.

25

"Man, damn! Don't you know nothing? I'm talkin' bout goin to the Y, the black gold, the hairy monster, some coochie pop. I'm talkin' 'bout getting some puss, man."

His words came out slurred.

"All right man, damn! I got yo' point." I pushed James away from my face, wiping his saliva off my cheek.

A guest at the party approached James and me with a lighted joint in his hand. I coughed as I fanned the smoke away.

The guest extended the joint in my direction, "Here you go, li'l man. Since you leaving fa' the military, I know you wanna get down. Go 'head, take a hit."

I looked at James briefly as if I were expecting some sort of approval. James remained quiet, awaiting my reaction.

"Oh, what the hell! I'll take a hit," I said, reaching for the joint.

Just as I was about to accept the handoff, James intercepted it.

He took a long puff and coughed briefly. "Will doesn't get high."

The party guest seemed to accept James' response and walked away, saying, "I heard that. Good luck, li'l man, I'll check ya later."

Surprised, I asked James, "Why didn't you want me smoking that joint?"

"'Cause I know you don't get high and I don't want you wastin' my friend's dope."

I knew his answer was untruthful. "Yeah, right. How would you know? You ain't been around."

Suddenly serious, he responded, "Look, li'l brother, I ain't gon' be there to protect you anymore. If you don't want to do drugs, don't say yes 'cause someone wants you to. Be strong enough to say no, and people will respect you for being strong enough to say so."

I couldn't believe what I was hearing. "You should listen to your own advice, James."

"Don't wanna say no. 'Sides, I can stop anytime I want," he said (of course).

James changed the subject abruptly by pointing to three girls sitting on the sofa, talking. The girls were snorting lines of cocaine and laughing uncontrollably.

"Look over there, Will. You see those three girls?"

"Yeah, what about 'em?"

"How'd ya like to get busy wit 'em?"

I shook my head in disapproval before answering, "Man, don't do me any favors. Those girls are ugly as sin, and drunker than Cooter Brown."

"Will, who in tha hell is Cooter Brown, anyway?"

"I don't know. Mama always says that when she sees somebody drunk."

James smiled. "I know she does, and so does everybody else in town. Don't worry 'bout how they look. Just have a few beers and they'll start to get mo' attractive."

James and I both laughed at his comment, until I noticed a young lady standing alone in the corner of the room.

I pointed in her direction. "James, who is that girl over there?"

James answered, "I don't know. I never seen her here before. Go over and say hello."

James gave me a slight nudge in her direction and I stumbled forward, wasting soda on my shirt. I turned to James and gave him the evil eye. He thought the large soda stain on my shirt was hilarious. I had hoped the young lady in the corner hadn't witnessed what happened. But as I turned to look at her, she was smiling after observing the incident. I wiped the stain off my shirt as best I could and walked over.

The young lady took a napkin and tried to wipe the stain away, "There you go, Will, that's looks much better."

Surprised that she knew my name, I said, "Thank you. You know my name, but I'm struggling to remember yours. Please forgive me."

"You mean you don't remember me from high school?"

"Oh, yeahhh. You're Michelle Montgomery, aren't you? You've changed so much since I last saw you. I don't mean that in a bad way. It's just that, man, you've become even more beautiful."

27

Michelle blushed, "Well now, thanks for the compliment."

"What in the world are you doing here?" I asked.

"My birthday is tomorrow and my friends talked me into hanging out tonight," she said.

"Where are your friends?"

Michelle pointed to the three girls snorting the cocaine. "Those three girls over there acting silly."

"Well, from what I remember about you in high school, it seems like we're both out of our element. What do you say me and you get outta here and go for a drive along the reservoir?" I suggested.

Michelle agreed. "Sounds great!"

I borrowed the convertible from James and we headed for the Ross Barnett reservoir in nearby Ridgeland. It was a hangout for most of the teenagers during that time. As we drove along the scenic route, I looked over at Michelle; we shared a smile as her hair blew in the breeze. I pulled over to a camping site located at the water's edge. I parked the car and turned off the engine.

"Well, here we are. There's a blanket in the trunk. You wanna sit on the hood?"

She smiled and said, "Sure. I don't mind."

I spread the blanket on the hood of the car and we climbed on. It was a clear night, with the moon's reflection beaming off the water. The only sound to be heard was thousands of gallons of water rushing through the nearby dam, and we felt the occasional mist on our face.

Michelle broke the silence. "This place is really beautiful!"

I nodded my head. "It's hard to believe that a place so beautiful could be named after someone as evil and racist as Ross Barnett."

"What do you mean?"

"My mother said that after Medgar Evers was killed, Barnett showed up in the courtroom to give support to Byron de la Beckwith, the guy who shot him. Ross Barnett and George Wallace are two governors the south will never forget."

There was momentary silence. I lay down on the hood, positioning my hands underneath my head.

Michelle asked, "Will, why didn't you notice me in high school? I had this enormous crush on you and I came to every one of your football games."

I was totally caught off guard. "Really! Hell, I never knew."

"I was even there the last game of our senior year when we played Pearl High for the championship. When you caught that pass in the last few seconds to win the game, I almost fainted. I ran on the field because I wanted a chance to hug and kiss you, but I couldn't get close enough. It seemed like everyone in the stands ran on to the field."

Michelle's comment brought a major smile to my face. I reminisced about one of the biggest rivalries in the state, and the greatest one-handed catch of my high school career.

I said to Michelle, "Man, I'll remember that night for the rest of my life! There must have been thousands of people on that field!"

Michelle lay down on the hood beside me, resting her head on my chest.

"Well, tonight, it's just me and you, Will. Can I finally have my chance?"

Scene 8

EXT—SAN ANTONIO, TEXAS—BASIC TRAINING

My day of departure for the Air Force finally came. That particular morning, my mother came to my room to help finish packing my bags. It was a sad day for her as well as myself.

My mother gave me last-minute advice: "You was always tha one that I neva' worried bout. 'Cause of tha grades you got in school and tha way that you hold yo' own with snooty people, I know you gon' succeed in whateva' you do. Remember yo' promise of treatin' all women wit respect, and always be a southern gentleman like I taught you."

Above all, my mother's most memorable words were, "Remember, Will, when yo' enemies attack you, kill 'em wit kindness."

I tried my best to convince her, "Don't worry, Mama, I can take care of myself."

I said good-bye to my mother that morning and she left for work in tears.

My father was leaving for work shortly thereafter.

I shook his hand and said good-bye, "Anythang else you need 'foe I leave?"

"Yes, there is one thing. From this day on, treat Mama with the respect that she deserves."

For what it was worth, my father assentingly nodded, then drove away.

James gave me a ride to the airport that morning. His eyes were bloodshot and his breath smelled of alcohol.

"Whew! Man, James, you smell like a distillery."

James gave me his usual smirk. "Rough night, li'l brother -- I had these two babes over. Was supposed to go ta work this morning but I was too damn tired."

I was not surprised by his answer, "Oh well, guess you lost another job, huh?"

James' only reply: "Whateva'!"

As we rode down the highway, we laughed and talked about our childhood days, especially the harsh times with our father. I

31

told James to keep in touch with our mother from time to time and make sure things were going all right with her; he gave me his assurance that he would. I tried to give James words of encouragement to help him get his life back in order, but I knew that he was enjoying the party type of lifestyle too much.

"What are your future plans, James?"

James ignored me as usual. He opened up the glove compartment and took out a joint. "My plan right now is to get high. I know you don't want any, right?"

"No, thanks! I'd like to keep my brain cells for a while."

"Will, what tha hell's the matta wit you man? You always been so serious 'bout life. You should learn ta relax more. Sometimes, I can't even believe we brothers."

James' comments pushed me to the verge of anger. "Instead of relaxing more, and looking at life as one big party, you should get more serious about life and responsibility. Can you name one friend that has something positive going on in their life?"

James paused briefly and seemed to search his mind. Then he abruptly changed the subject. "Stop tryin' ta preach to me, li'l brother!"

My tour of duty in the Air Force started in San Antonio, Texas, with basic training, and I can still remember the intense heat.. Unlike Mississippi, where you can't tell your sweat and the wet air apart, Texas heat makes you want to sweat to prove you haven't suffocated.

Military basic training is something anyone fortunate enough to experience it never forgets. I knew from my first encounter with the military training instructor *(Taylor, you better pray that God takes your soul, cause for the next six weeks your sweet ass belongs to me....)* that I had some serious mental preparing to do for what lay ahead.

In the long six weeks of basic training, getting noticed is not something you want to do. The best way to get through it is by keeping quiet, following orders without questioning them, and keeping your appearance neat.

I became friends with most of the guys in the unit. The distinctions of race and background fall away when everyone faces the same adversity together.

About fifty men of widely diverse backgrounds were assigned to my unit. Some guys were there on the *buddy system* -- you joined the Air Force with a friend and you both went through the training process at the same time.

The guys in the unit came from all over: besides San Antonio and other parts of the state, they came from California, New York, and even Hawaii. Two guys from South Dakota seemed to keep to themselves the first couple of weeks. As time went on, they began to open up to the rest of the group. It turned out that being around people of color was new to them. Therefore, they were uncomfortable and didn't want anyone to find out. Since we were close to our last week of basic training, no one in the group was offended. By now, everyone in the group had shared some kind of secret or story about their hometown.

The story that I shared was about the monument of the Confederate soldier. I also told how the blacks lived on one side of town and the whites lived on the other. Most of the guys couldn't believe that, in this year of 1982, people in the South still lived that way.

The sixth and final week of my basic training finally came. We were now the so-called seniors on the block, supposedly the most polished and elite, ready for a career in the United States Air Force. We marched everywhere in our dress uniform. All the groups of new recruits looked at us in envy, wondering whether they could survive to one day wear that dress uniform. As we passed the new recruits, my thoughts reverted back to the first days after my arrival, and I thanked God for getting me through.

Graduation day finally arrived and it was one of the proudest days of my life. I felt a great sense of accomplishment. Most of my group successfully completed basic training. However, about ten didn't make it: they couldn't follow orders, hadn't passed physical performance standards, or had admitted to homosexuality.

During that time, being gay in the military was unacceptable. No one really knew whether the guys were gay or were just looking for a way out of basic training. Not that it mattered, though. Once you became associated with the term *homosexual*, you were on your way out of the military.

Some of the guys' parents and friends came to San Antonio for the graduation. I wished my mother was there but I knew she couldn't afford to attend.

As soon as the graduation was over, I ran to a pay phone to call home and share my accomplishments with the family. As I waited in the booth, I hoped my mother would answer. She was the first person I wanted to share my good news with. I got my wish and blurted out the news, and she shared my excitement. Finally, I asked about the rest of the family.

"Yo' father continues ta come home in his mad-at-tha-world attitude, and yo' brother is still livin tha party life."

My excitement faded. My mother offered more words of praise and encouragement to help me face my new military career before we said goodbye, and I tried to get the spirit of the day back. But that was only the start of how the trouble back home would shadow me throughout my federal career.

Scene 9

INT—SMALL TOWN JAILHOUSE—BRANDON, MISSISSIPPI

After completing Air Traffic Control training, I was able to get a few days off before heading to my new duty station in St. Louis, Missouri. I was headed home and excited about finally seeing my family again, especially Mama. It had been six months.

As I drove down the gravel road leading to my parent's house, I could see my parents walking across the front lawn, carrying what looked like brown, paper grocery bags. As I drove the rental car closer and closer, my parents struggled to identify the visitor driving the unfamiliar car. They both stood silently, gazing at the car until I stopped in the driveway.

I stepped out of the car in my Air Force uniform, smiling like Stevie Wonder. My mother dropped the bags of groceries and ran toward me, screaming, with outstretched arms. Remembering how James teased her on his return from Germany, I evaded her by running around the front yard in circles with her giving chase. When she began to tire, I stopped running and approached her. She embraced me with a bone-crushing hug.

"Boy, what are you doin' home? Why didn't ya tell me you were comin'?"

I wiped the tears away from her cheeks, "I wanted to surprise you, Mama. 'Sides, I didn't want you counting the days."

Still overcome, she asked, "How long ya here for?"

"Just for a couple of days. I have to get to my new duty station in St. Louis."

My father and I made eye contact. He walked over, slowly extending his hand. "Welcome home, fly boy. How thangs goin'?"

I shook his hand. "Not bad. I can't complain."

My mother interrupted, "St. Louis, that sho is a long ways from home."

"It's not that far away, Mama. It's only about an eight-hour drive. Even shorter if you fly."

35

My mother placed her hands on her hip and gave me the you-know-better look, "Will, you know I ain't g'tting' on no plane, so I guess you'll be comin' to see me."

My father couldn't fight his curiosity any longer. He asked, "Will, whose car you drivin'?"

"It's a rental car, Daddy. I rented it for a couple of days."

Somewhat envious, he said, "It sho' is nice. How you 'fford that?"

I reached into my front left pant pocket and pulled out a wad of cash.

"I saved up, plus Uncle Sam gave me traveling money to get to St. Louis."

"Damn, must be nice," my father replied as he turned away and walked into the house.

I shook my head at his response. My mother offered an apology for my comment. "Don't pay yo' father no mind, you know how he is. Come on, help me get these groceries in the house."

My mother and I put the groceries away and conversed for most of the afternoon. It seemed as if we had a million things to catch up on. I eventually ended up in the family room, hoping to catch a quick nap, while she prepared dinner. I lay down on the sofa, yawned, and had barely closed my eyes when the telephone rang.

I picked up the phone. "Hello?"

There was momentary silence, and then, "Hey, who is this?"

Recognizing James' voice, I said, "How quickly they forget."

"Will! Man, what you doin' home?"

"I'm home for a few days before headin' to St. Louis. You coming over or what?"

"I would love to, li'l brother, but I got arrested last night for D.W.I. Was just callin' for Mama to come and post bail."

I sighed. "I can see some things haven't changed."

I must have struck a nerve. "Look, man, I ain't in tha mood fa one of yo' righteous sermons! Just give Mama tha message!"

"How much is bail, James?" I hesitantly asked.

"Don't know, maybe six or seven hundred dollars," James said carelessly.

"Fool, are you crazy? Where you think Mama's gon' get that kinda money?"

Like so many times before, James hadn't considered the consequences of his actions. "I don't know. Maybe she can borrow it."

I responded, "Here's an idea. Why don't you call some of yo' broke-ass friends and ask them for the money?"

"Just tell Mama, damn it," James yelled before slamming the phone down.

At that moment, I despised him. My mother had enough hard times and disappointments in her life; she didn't need him putting her through more. I was all set to surprise her by coming home for a week, but now she would have to deal with my brother being arrested.

I thought about the devastation that my brother's arrest would have on her, both emotionally and financially. I decided that this was one heartache I would spare her.

My mother came in and saw me still holding the telephone.

"Who was that, Will?"

"Huh? Oh, that was Michelle. She wants me to come over."

My mother smiled and said, "I see. You just gettin' in town and chasing girls already."

I've never liked the idea of lying to my mother, but it seemed best. "What can I say? It's been a long six months. I'll be back later tonight. Don't wait up."

I headed for the small-town jailhouse with all the money that I had saved, along with the money that I had received for travel to St. Louis. I hoped it was enough to post my brother's bail.

Upon arriving at the jail, an obese, middle-aged desk sergeant was reading a magazine, leaning back in his chair with his feet on the desk. He had a wad of tobacco in his cheek and leaned over to spit into a brown-stained cup before he spoke.

"What ya need?"

I glanced at the large Confederate flag occupying the space on the wall behind him, then nervously answered, "I'm here to post bail."

"And who might dat be for?"

"Taylor."

The desk sergeant leaned over and spat into the brown stained cup again, partially missing. "Ol' James. Yeah, he in our country club. I'm sorry, James don' did it this time. Less you got a thousand dollars, I'm 'fraid he gon' be our guest for a while. So you best be on yo' way."

With a sarcastic smile, the desk sergeant resumed reading his magazine. He obviously assumed that a kid my age would definitely not have a thousand dollars and would therefore surely be on the way out the door and out of his hair.

I took the large wad of cash from my pocket, "Is it okay if I pay in cash?"

He slammed his magazine down on the desk and stood up. His face took on the shade of an over-ripened tomato. He watched me count out the ten one hundred-dollar bills with a cold stare.

"Where tha hell did a young boy like you get a thousand dollars?"

I remembered the advice my mother had given James and me: "If ya ever have a conversation wit the police, always keep a cool head, no matta how much they provoke you."

My mother told us countless stories of how black people in town were provoked to the point of being arrested and then sometimes beaten up in jail. I stood there silently, not saying a word.

"I ask you a question, boy," he yelled.

Once the desk sergeant realized that he wasn't going to provoke a response, he angrily processed my brother's paperwork.

The sergeant yelled to the jailer in the back, "Bring out Taylor!"

He filled out a receipt for the thousand dollars I'd just given him, crumpled it up, and threw it at me. I assumed that he was still hoping to provoke me. I bent over slowly, picked up the receipt, and placed it in my pocket.

The jailer escorted James down the hall. As James came closer, I could see that he was holding his head down and walking with a limp. The jailer took the handcuffs off.

The desk sergeant said, "Ya free ta go, James, but I got a feelin' I be seeing you again."

Raising his head, James looked at me, "What's up, li'l brother?"

His face was swollen and his left eye had a pretty good shiner.

I turned to the desk sergeant. "What happened to my brother's face?"

The desk sergeant returned to his seat before answering. "Yo' brother was drivin' while intoxicated. When we was arrestin' him, he fell down while gettin outta tha car. Ain't that right, James?"

I gave the desk sergeant a look of disbelief, and pounded my fist on the desk, "Whatever you say. I guess it takes a big man to hit a guy in handcuffs!"

After a brief stare down with the desk sergeant, I helped James out the door and into the car. "Man, am I'm glad to see you, Will!"

"I'm taking you to the hospital," I said.

"Naw, you ain't. Where Mama get the bail money this time?"

"I didn't tell her anything about this, James. How did you end up in jail?"

"I don't wanna talk about it right now. I just wanna go home and rest."

When we arrived at James' apartment, I helped him inside and to his bedroom. I helped him undress because he wasn't able to do it himself. After getting him to bed, I made sure that he wasn't in need of anything else. Before I left, he made me promise that I wouldn't tell Mama of his condition.

"Hey, man, don't tell Mama 'bout this. And thanks a lot for squaring me away, I owe ya."

"You damn right you owe me. You owe me big time!"

I arrived back at my parent's house and found my mother asleep in the faded recliner in the family room. She awakened when I walked through the door. I entered the room and sat on the sofa.

I whispered, "Why are you still up, Mama?"

She yawned and smiled before answering, "I couldn't sleep. I'm too excited 'bout you being home. You see James tonight?"

Remembering the lie that I told my mother earlier, and knowing that she was unaware of the *Dear John* letter that I had received a few weeks earlier from Michelle, I replied, "Yep, before I went to Michelle's house."

"I'm glad that girl finally got a chance ta see you. When you first left home, every time I saw that girl in town she was always askin' bout you."

"I guess she didn't miss me too much. She told me she's been dating someone else."

My mother laughed while clapping her hands. "I knew that already. Ain't nothin' secret in this li'l town. I wanted to tell ya but I decided to let her tell ya herself. 'Sides, you thank you somethin special and dat girl just gon' sit round and wait on you?"

Somewhat embarrassed, I answered, "I guess not."

My mother tried to smoothe things over. "Baby, don't worry 'bout it. You gon' find you one 'a dem pretty St. Louis girls that'll put these li'l country girls to shame. So, how's James doin'?"

"He's all right, Mama."

"Well, I'm worried 'bout him. I think he maybe using drugs. Seem like every since he came from the army..." she yawned before she could finish her sentence.

"Mama, you been givin him money?"

"'A course. I help pay his rent and some other bills. You know I'll always help either 'a you boys out who needs it."

Not surprised by her answer, I asked the question that I really didn't want an answer to: "How many times you bail him out of jail, Mama?"

My mother yawned again, closed her eyes, and tilted her head back against the recliner, "James is a good boy, he gonna straighten up. You'll see."

Scene 10

EXT/INT—JAMES' TRAILER HOME—FRONT LAWN/BEDROOM

I began my aviation career with the 131st Tactical Fighter Squadron located at St. Louis International Airport. The squadron took pride in calling itself "Lindbergh's Own." It was home base for a squadron of F-4E jet aircraft and the pilots who flew them. The F-4E's were somewhat aged, and the mechanics faced major problems in keeping them operational for flight. A good portion of the flights normally ended with the pilot declaring some type of emergency on their return to the traffic pattern at St. Louis airport.

My job at flight operations centered mainly on flight scheduling, filing the aircrews flight plans, and keeping track of aircraft departures and arrivals. I loved my job and it was the first time that I had felt effective in my life in a long time.

My first four years of enlistment were coming to an end and I had already signed up for another four-year hitch. By now, I had purchased a new BMW and was sharing a nice bachelor pad with my best friend, Bobby, who was also in the military.

My brother James had progressively gotten worse over the years. He eventually lost his apartment and spent most of his time now living with different women.

I hadn't been home for a couple years and I was tired of the dating scene in St. Louis, so I decided to take some time off and drive down South to see my mother.

Brandon hadn't changed much with the exception of a few new stores. Unsurprisingly, the monument of the Confederate soldier still held its post right in the heart of town. Its presence reminded me that this small town was still a world apart from the rest of the country.

I arrived at my parents' house that Friday at about 7 p.m. As I pulled into the gravel driveway, I could see the silhouette of someone pulling the curtain aside, looking out the window. I got out of the car and walked toward the front door. I had taken only a few steps before the front door flew open, and out ran my mother screaming with excitement. As usual, I ran around the yard in circles avoiding her. As always, when I realized Mama was getting tired, I stopped running and braced myself for one of her breathtaking hugs.

"Will, when I catch my breath.....I'm gon' put you cross my knee. Boy, what in tha world you doin home?"

"I had a few days off and decided to come see you."

"Did you drive all tha way from St. Louis?" my mother asked as she averted her attention to my new car.

"Yep, took about eight hours. How you like my new car?"

My mother has always had a way of putting things in perspective. To this day, she has never driven a car and therefore puts little emphasis on any particular vehicle, American made or foreign.

Pointing at the car, I asked, "Do you like it? It's a BMW."

"A what?" she answered.

"A BMW. A German car."

She looked at the car again and said in her own sweet way, "It's cute, and kinda shiny!"

I looked at my mother and laughed. Her comment made me glad to be home and realize why I loved her so much.

My father stood in the front doorway, somewhat envious of all the excitement between my mother and me.

"Pops, how ya doing?"

My father responded, " I'm doin fine, Will. From the looks of that new car, you doin' a lot betta than me. Wish I could 'fford a car like that."

I looked at my mother. "It's just a car, Daddy. It ain't no big deal."

"If you can 'fford a car like that, then maybe you oughta be sending some money home to me and yo' Mama."

My mother stepped in to diffuse a potential argument, "Leave the boy alone, we ain't hurtin' fa' nothin'. He just gettin' home and you messin' wit him already!"

"Well, maybe if you wasn't givin' all yo' money ta James, we have mo' 'round the house," my father said before heading back into the house.

My mother embraced me again. "Don't pay him no mind, baby. You know how yo' father is. We doin' just fine, C'mon in the house."

I sat around and talked with my mother for a couple of hours. My father remained mostly quiet, interjecting a few words every now and then.

My mother wasted no time inquiring about my personal life. "How thangs been in St. Louis? You and Bobby still chasing all them St. Louis girls?"

"St. Louis is great, and Bobby is doing all right. I'm kinda fed up with the dating scene; I'm just taking a break for a while."

"Will, ya probably tryin' to hard. When ya meet someone truly special, you'll know it."

"I hear ya, Mama. So, how's James doing?"

My mother hesitated. Her expression changed from delight to sadness. "Ya brother ain't been doin' so good. Since James got evicted from his apartment, he been livin wit different girls off and on. Half the time I don't even know where he is. He spend most his time drinkin' and using drugs. I'm 'fraid he gon' turn up dead somewhere."

I smiled and said, "Mama, don't worry about it. I'll track him down and have a talk with him."

In a small town like Brandon, it was hard to keep secrets. After visiting some old friends, it wasn't long before I learned where James was staying. He lived with a young girl on the outskirts of town, in a trailer home that she had inherited from a deceased aunt.

The area where my brother lived was nothing short of horrible. I drove down the narrow dirt road past several vacant lots full of trash. Abandoned cars littered the roadside. The houses only seemed to be hanging together by a nail.

I arrived in the front yard of the trailer and several stray dogs announced me. I got of the car and approached the front porch. The sound of the dogs must have caught the attention of someone inside because the front door began to open. A petite woman appeared from behind the door. She appeared to be quite young and, as I walked toward her, I could tell that she was afraid. I introduced myself and told her that I was looking for my brother, James.

She introduced herself. "I'm Gwen. James told me all about you. You can come in. He in tha bedroom."

"Thank you," I said as I stepped inside.

I gave a smile to a little girl, presumably Gwen's daughter, sitting in a high chair in the small kitchen. Gwen led me down the short hall to the bedroom, opening the door slowly. There sat James in the corner of the room. Although it had been a while since we'd seen each other, the scene was all too familiar. James was smoking a joint, drinking malt liquor, and watching a pornographic movie on the television. Upon seeing me, he was so surprised that he was speechless. I approached James with outstretched arms. He stood and attempted to walk toward me, but stumbled from the effects of the alcohol and marijuana.

We embraced. I smiled and said to him, "I see some things haven't changed!"

James gave me his patented sarcastic look. "I guess not, 'cause you still tryin to preach to me, Reverend Taylor."

Gwen left the room, closing the door behind her. James sat down in the recliner and I sat on the edge of the bed.

"What's been going on with your life, big brother?"

James took a hit from the joint, coughing briefly before answering. "Man, shit. It seem like everythang's been goin' down hill for me. You know I got evicted from my apartment right?"

"Oh really, how'd that happen?"

Taking a sip of malt liquor, he said, "Late on rent a couple times; some of tha neighbors callin' the cops a couple times when I was havin' my Friday night parties, talkin' 'bout the music was too loud. You know how it is, white folks don't want a brother havin' nothin' in this small town."

Just like my father, James liked to blame other people for his shortcomings.

Always trying to practice tough love with James, I said, "Oh, really! Is it the white folks' fault that you drinking all the time and smoking dope?"

44

My response must have hit a little bit too close to home. James set the joint in an ashtray, and the bottle of malt liquor on the floor.

His voice rose a few decibels. "Will, why you always comin' down on me, man? I'm still yo' big brother no matta what I do!"

I put my hand on James' knee, and we stared at each other momentarily.

"I guess you right, big brother. It's just that I don't want to see you throw your life away."

I figured it best to change the subject, "You know Mama's been worried about you. How come you don't go see her more?"

"I know I should. I just can't take much of yo Daddy's mouth these days."

Glancing out the bedroom window, James noticed my car, "Damn, is that yo new car?"

"Just got it a few months ago."

James stood and stumbled toward the bedroom door. "C'mon. Let's go take a look."

We made our way to the front lawn, with the stray dogs providing the sound effects again.

James chased them away by throwing a few stones, connecting once or twice. "Get outta here, ya mangy ass mutts."

"Come on, man, leave those dogs alone," I said, laughing and opening the car's front door.

"I hate dem damn dogs," James said as he smiled and looked inside.

"A BMW. Man, this sucka sho' is nice. I bet you getting a lot of St. Louis women with this ride, huh?"

"I do all right. Been kinda bored, just takin a break for a while."

"Shit! Man, if that was me, I be runnin' ho'es left and right!"

I gave James a sarcastic look, shaking my head. "Somehow I believe you would. By the way, who is this young girl you stayin' with?"

"Just some li'l freak I turned out. She only seventeen. Shit, this trailer is hers. Her aunt died and left it to her. It's all right for tha time being."

My brother seemed to be doing all right so I decided to move on, "Well, it looks like you're in good spirits. I think I'll go and visit some old friends."

James said, "Go head. They doin' the same thang they was when you left home fo' years ago. Ain't nothin to do in this lil town."

"I hear ya. What you want me to tell Mama and Daddy?"

"You can tell yo big-head Daddy to kiss my ass! But tell Mama I'll be callin' her soon."

"I'll do it," I said, smiling after James' response, "You take care."

James and I embraced. Then he said, "Don't worry 'bout me, li'l brother. I'll be all right."

Scene 11

INT—MONTAGUE HOME—ST. LOUIS, MISSOURI

Although my time off was well appreciated, I was glad to be back in St. Louis. Just seeing my mother's face again had made my trip worthwhile. It was Saturday morning; I sat on the sofa in my apartment watching the Lakers and the Bulls go after each other. *Jordan* and *Magic* were putting on a basketball clinic as usual.

My roommate, Bobby, darted out of his bedroom holding a cordless phone, wearing only his underwear and tube socks.

Bobby was very excited, "It's on, Jerome! It's on, baby," he said while trying to restrain himself.

Noticing the way that he was dressed, I couldn't resist the opportunity, "Judging by the way you're dressed, along with that big smile on your face, it looks like you're enjoying yourself in your room. What's up with that?"

Bobby displayed a look of sarcasm and flipped me the bird, "I just hooked up with Tracy and made plans for the night. She was going to hang out with her friend Lisa, but I persuaded her to let us come along."

I shook my head. "Ohhh, no! I helped you out last time. I'm not falling for that blind-date-with-the-ugly-friend thing again."

"C'mon Will, it's cool this time. I've seen pictures and she's fine. Trust me."

"Right! I heard that line before."

"You ain't had a date in a while anyway, so I know...you gotta be a li'l horny. Come on, room-dog, it'll be fun."

Bobby seemed to really have his hopes up and was looking forward to finally getting a date with Tracy. He was my best friend and I didn't want to let him down. Reluctantly, I agreed, and a few hours later we dressed and headed out for the infamous Blind Date.

We arrived at Tracy's a short time later. She greeted us and invited us in until she finished getting dressed. Tracy was nothing short of beautiful, and bore a striking resemblance to

Whitney Houston. Needless to say, she definitely met with Bobby's approval.

She telephoned Lisa to let her know that we were on the way and then we were out the door. Bobby fired up the Saab and we were off to pick up "the ugly friend." I was curious about her friend Lisa, and the conversation in the car centered mostly around how she and Lisa had become friends.

We had been riding for about forty-five minutes when Bobby asked Tracy the question that was on my mind as well. "Damn, Tracy. Where in the hell does Lisa live, Kansas?"

I echoed Bobby's thoughts, "Yeah, Tracy, where the hell are we?"

Tracy laughed, "We're almost there. There, turn into that subdivision."

We turned into a very affluent subdivision. From the rearview mirror, Bobby glanced at me with eyes wide and eyebrows raised. I gave him the same look back.

Tracy pointed to a large, three-story house at the end of the street. "There's Lisa's house at the end of the cul-de-sac. Park in the driveway."

We got out of the car and headed for the front door. Bobby and I looked at each other again in disbelief as Tracy walked slightly in front of us. I started to think I was out of my league and that Lisa's parents surely would not approve of a small-town country boy looking to spend time with their daughter.

Tracy rang the doorbell and Lisa's mother greeted us at the door. Lisa's mother was a stunning, middle-aged woman who conveyed class from head to toe.

Tracy greeted Lisa's mother with an embrace, and we were then ushered into the large foyer. The house was unlike anything that I'd ever seen. The contemporary decor and expensive furnishings mirrored images I'd only read about in novels as a kid. Having grown up poor in a small town, I'd experienced white people with nice homes, but nothing that could hold a candle to this one.

Tracy introduced us. "Mrs. Montague, this is Bobby Fletcher and Will Taylor."

"Hello, Bobby, I'm Carol Montague."

Mrs. Montague stretched out her hand to greet Bobby, but he never saw it. He was too busy walking around the foyer trying to get a closer look at the expensive furnishings.

Bobby went into his usual bullshit mode right away, "Damn, Tracy, you didn't tell me they were Buppies. I mean, I didn't know black folks lived like this."

Bobby's comment obviously offended Mrs. Montague, as you could see her cheekbones tighten and a small wrinkle appear in her forehead. I sighed silently and tried to smoothe over the situation.

I took Mrs. Montague's hand, averting her attention, "Mrs. Montague, please excuse Bobby; it's not his fault. He is the result of years of in-breeding."

"Well, keep him on a tight leash when he meets my husband," she said.

Unfortunately, Bobby wasn't done with his snide comments, "Sorry ma'am, I'm just in awe. In my neighborhood, we call this a hotel."

Mrs. Montague approached Bobby, waving her finger. Just as she was about to let him have what I imagine was a great piece of her mind, Lisa's father entered the foyer, from down the hall.

"Which one of you wants to date my daughter?" he said in an intimidating tone of voice.

Mr. Montague was a muscular man whose 6'4" frame towered over us. I looked up at him and stretched my hand to meet his.

I said nervously, "Will Taylor, sir."

Our hands met; we stared into each other's eyes and shook hands. This was the first time that I had met someone with a handshake that was considerably stronger than mine.

His hand dwarfed mine, and he possessed the type of handshake that demanded respect. "Ron Montague. Lisa tells me you're from Mississippi."

"Yes, sir, a very small town named Brandon."

"So, where's your southern accent?"

"Growing up, I worked hard on my diction. My friends teased me a lot and said I sounded white. Whatever that means."

"I can relate to some of that myself. Grew up in a poverty-stricken area of St. Louis' inner city. Sometimes the price you pay for success is the loss of family, or so-called friends."

Our conversation was interrupted as Mrs. Montague alerted Lisa to our arrival.

"Lisa, they're here," she called up from the base of the huge stairwell.

The butterflies that I hadn't realized were in my stomach took flight. I searched for the right words to say when she appeared. A thought came to mind of a conversation that I had had with my mother. Once when I was in high school, I had tried desperately to win a girl's affection, but she wasn't having it.

My mother's advice was, "Just be yourself, Will, 'cause most girls can see right through a smoke screen. Be that southern gentleman that I always taught you to be."

Two high school aged girls appeared at the top of the stairs, giggling uncontrollably.

"Where's your sister?" Mrs. Montague asked.

At that moment, another young woman appeared suddenly from an upstairs bedroom. She paused momentarily at the top of the stairs, as if she were a model at a photo shoot. Her smile lit up the whole foyer, and I thought she was the prettiest girl I'd ever seen. As she walked down the stairs slowly, I stared in amazement, watching her every move.

Mrs. Montague said, "Here's Lisa. Lisa, this is Will."

Lisa stretched her hand out, awaiting mine for a handshake. I took Lisa's hand, looked into her eyes, and gently kissed it. "It's truly a pleasure to meet you."

Lisa smiled and looked nervously at Tracy and her parents. I was afraid that kissing her hand had made her uneasy. "I'm sorry. I hope I didn't make you feel uncomfortable."

Blushing, she said, "No, it's just that most guys don't kiss hands."

"Southern gentlemen always do when they meet a beautiful lady."

"Are you really a southern gentleman?" she asked.

I smiled and raised her hand to my lips again, "Do you want me to kiss your hand again?"

50

Mr. Montague was quick to intervene, "No! There's no need for that," he said sternly as he pulled my hand away from Lisa's.

Lisa smacked her father on the shoulder, "Daddy...! Well, I hope he hasn't been interrogating you too much."

I assured Lisa that everything was fine and we prepared to leave. Lisa pointed up the stairs in the direction of the two girls, who were taking in all the action and still giggling uncontrollably.

"Those are my two brain-damaged little sisters, Lori and Heather."

I smiled and waved, "Hello, ladies," before turning my attention to Mr. Montague.

"It was a pleasure meeting you, Mr. Montague. I hope to see you again, sir."

Mr. Montague shrugged and said, "Don't forget, Lisa has a curfew."

As we left the house and headed for Bobby's car, I tried to ease the mood by commenting to Lisa, "I had no idea you lived this far away. Next time, I think I'll pack a lunch."

Lisa didn't hesitate to put me in check, "Oh, really. And what makes you think there will be a next time?"

INT—WILL AND BOBBY'S APARTMENT— (BLINDDATE)

Tracy, Bobby, Lisa, and I sat on the sofas in our apartment, checking out the movie we 'd rented. We laughed and talked throughout the movie until it ended.

Bobby stood and stretched, "Hey, Tracy, let's break out and give my room-dog some space to maneuver. How 'bout a drive downtown?"

"What about Lisa?" she asked Bobby.

"Will's got a car. He can take Lisa home. This time he can drive all the way to Kansas!"

Lisa smirked at Bobby's comment, "Ha, ha, Bobby, very funny."

Bobby looked at me. "You don't mind, do you, Will?"

Tracy and I looked at Lisa for approval. "Is that all right with you?" Tracy asked.

Lisa responded, "Will has seen the size of my father; I think I'll be alright."

"You got that right. He's as big as a Mississippi oak," I said..

That's all Bobby needed to hear. "Good. Let's get outta here, Tracy."

Bobby and Tracy left the apartment, and I walked into the kitchen and opened the refrigerator.

"Well, let's see. Here's a bottle of Asti. Would you like some?"

"Sure, sounds great," Lisa said.

I popped the cork on the champagne, walked over to the bar, and filled two glasses. I made my way over to the stereo and selected a CD from the collection. Soft music played in the background, and I returned to my seat on the sofa beside Lisa. She observed every move.

I handed her a glass of champagne, and she couldn't resist commenting, "Well now, looks like you've done this before, Mr. Taylor."

Taken aback, I gave a short laugh. "Not often. I'm nervous as hell, to be honest. Just making it up as I go along."

"Yeah, right. You expect me to believe that?"

Lisa and I continued to talk for a few more hours. We began to realize how much we had in common.

I told her about my past dating experiences. "I'm just fed up with dating. The mind games, the senseless relationships."

To my surprise, she'd had similar experiences. "Yeah, I've been on hiatus myself. My last relationship didn't work out. I guess I finally realized you can't make someone be something they're not."

I gently took her hand and placed it between both of mine.

I leaned forward, positioning myself closer, and whispered, "Lisa, there is one thing that I do know."

"And what might that be, Mr. Taylor?" she asked with a smile.

"Whoever the guy is that let you slip away, he's the biggest fool in St. Louis. If you were mine, I would spoil you and treat you like the queen that you are."

We gazed into each other's eyes and the mood turned quite serious.

"Are you sure, Will? Would you care for me that much?"

"Lisa, I've never been so sure about anything, or anyone, in my life."

Hesitantly, Lisa said, "Somehow, I really believe you would."

Lisa and I kissed passionately on the sofa. It was one of the deepest kisses that I've ever experienced, and my heart felt on the verge of exploding. Minutes later, she pushed me away and we both stood immediately.

"Whew-whee! I think you better be taking me home right about now," she said, rubbing the back of her neck.

"Whew man, I think you're right. We got a little carried away!"

I retrieved our coats from the closet. I assisted Lisa with her coat and she turned around to face me. We found ourselves face to face, staring in each other's eyes again. I placed my hands on her waist and pulled her even closer. She placed her arms around my neck at the same time as if it was an instant reflex. We began to kiss passionately again, and this time I could feel her trembling in my arms. I knew that she wanted me as much as I wanted her.

I'm not a superstitious person, nor do I know whether the idea of a soul mate deserves credence. However, as of that night, I knew that this lady would one day be my wife and the mother of my children.

Scene 13

INT—"4 STAR" RESTAURANT—ST. LOUIS

During the next few months, Lisa and I were inseparable. Our friends became envious to the point of calling us henpecked, whipped, and whatever else they could think of. We couldn't get enough of each other. Although I had known Lisa only for a few months, I felt as if she were the woman for whom I had waited a lifetime.

A new black-tie restaurant had recently opened in downtown St. Louis, and I was lucky enough to score some reservations. I couldn't wait to call and tell Lisa the news.

I greeted her on the phone with "Hi, babe, what ya doing?"

Always glad to hear from me, she said, "Just lying here thinking of you."

"Good. That's the way it should be. What are you doing this Saturday night?"

"I don't have any special plans, but if you do, I hope they include me."

"Have I got a surprise for you! I have dinner reservations at that new fancy restaurant downtown."

Excited, she refused to believe me. "No way! Their waiting list is always a mile long. My parents have been trying to get reservations there for months. They're going to freak!"

Luckily, one of the pilots I worked with ran a limousine business on the side and had a contract with the restaurant to shuttle customers back and forth. The pilot, John, was a good friend of the co-owner.

I wouldn't divulge my inside connection to Lisa and it drove her crazy.

I was finally able to change the subject. "So, Ms. Montague, I assume you want to go?"

"Are you serious? I'd love to!"

"Great! The reservations are for seven-thirty. I'll pick you up at six."

That Saturday, I counted the hours until it was finally show time. The tuxedo that I had rented a few days earlier fit great, and as I struggled with the bowtie, my roommate, Bobby, took great pleasure in giving me grief.

"Damn, Will, two months and this girl has you renting a tux and spending money at expensive restaurants. Lisa's got your nose opened so wide, you can't even see your tie. Here, let me tie it."

I laughed and handed the tie to Bobby allowing him to do the honor. "You can say what you want Bob, but this lady is the one I've been waiting for. Besides, you're just envious because your dating criteria isn't any higher than farm animals."

"Yeah, yeah, whatever Will," Bobby answered as he finished, "Get outta here, you're going to be late."

I arrived at Lisa's on schedule and rang the doorbell. I brushed away a few pieces of lint while waiting for someone to open the door. Mrs. Montague appeared, gave me a hug, and invited me in.

"Hi, Will. You look very nice tonight. C'mon in -- Lisa is just about ready."

"Thank you, ma'am. I'll just wait here in the foyer."

"Nonsense! Go have a seat in the family room with Ron," she said, and escorted me down the hall.

Mr. Montague sat in a recliner watching television.

He stood to greet me. "Will, what's happening, man? You look clean as a whistle."

The compliment meant a lot coming from a man of his stature, and I was very appreciative. "Thank you sir."

"Lisa tells me you guys are headed to that new restaurant downtown. How'd you get reservations?"

"I guess I was just lucky sir."

"I've been trying to get reservations to that place for the past two months. Tried to cash in favors from everyone, including the mayor."

Mrs. Montague interrupted our short conversation.

From the foyer, she said, "Okay, Will, she's ready."

Mr. Montague and I walked down the hall and joined his wife at the base of the stairwell.

Mrs. Montague pointed to the top of the stairs. Lisa stood there with the prettiest smile that I had ever seen. She was dressed in a long, black evening gown with sequins that glistened with her every move, accentuated by a large diamond necklace and earrings. Her hair was perfect, without a single strand out of place.

She started her descent down the stairs and her mother playfully announced her arrival: *"Will Taylor, I present to you Ms. Lisa Montague!"*

I was captivated by her every move. When she reached the base of the stairs, we embraced and I said, "Lisa, you look extremely beautiful."

"Thank you," she answered, "You always know the right things to say."

Mrs. Montague took out a camera. "Big smile."

The camera flashed and everyone broke out in laughter. I said to Lisa, "We'd better get going. Don't want to be late."

Lisa said farewell to her parents and her father dropped some last minute advice. "Lisa, don't forget about your curfew. You guys have been pushing it lately."

I assured her father, "I'll make sure she's home on time tonight, sir."

Mr. Montague's attitude turned serious. He placed his right hand on my shoulder and warned, "Son....you make damn sure you do."

We were on our way and arrived at the four-star restaurant fifteen minutes early. It was candlelight dining and all the couples were dressed in elegant attire. The mood was captivating as soft piano music filled the air.

The maitre d' approached us. "Yes?" he inquired.

I responded, "Taylor."

The maitre d' seemed skeptical. "You have reservations here, sir?"

"That's correct," I said, and handed him the reservations.

He read the reservation and gave us a cold stare. "Just a minute, sir. I'll be right back."

Lisa turned to face me with a look of disappointment, "Will, what's the problem?"

"Oh it's evident what the problem is, but just calm down, babe. One thing my mother taught me growing up in Brandon is to always remain cool; never panic too early."

The maitre d' returned with the manager.

"Sir, this is the couple," the maitre d' said.

The manager said, "Hello, may I be of assistance?"

I handed the tickets to the manager, "We have reservations for seven-thirty."

The manager looked at the reservations briefly, then smiled.

"Of course, you're John's friend from flight operations. He speaks quite highly of you, and I can see why in your selection of such a beautiful date."

Lisa smiled, thanking him for the compliment. "Why thank you; you're very kind."

The manager apologized, "I'm truly sorry for any inconvenience. Please let me show you to your table."

The manager turned to the maitre d' with a look of anger, "Didn't you see the signature on the reservation, you jackass!"

I winked at the maitre d' as we followed the manager to our table. Although Lisa and I attracted stares from most of the couples, nothing was going to ruin that night for us. When we reached our table, I pulled Lisa's chair out and helped her be seated.

After I seated myself, the manager said, "Will, Lisa, let me know if there's anything else I can do for you."

We both said thanks and he walked away glaring at the maitre d' from across the room.

"Well, I'm glad that little drama's over," I said to Lisa as I tried to relax.

"Let's don't let it spoil our night, okay?" she said after taking a deep breath.

I tried to change the mood. "So, what do you think?"

Lisa looked around the restaurant, taking in the scenery. "It's lovely. I can see why it's so hard to get reservations."

Feeling as if all eyes were upon us, I tried to ease the tension. "Is it just me, Lisa, or does everyone in here look like they're over fifty years old?"

It appeared to work to some extent, as we both shared a laugh.

The waiter arrived carrying a bottle of champagne. "Hello, how are we doing tonight? The manager sent over this bottle of champagne with his compliments."

The waiter popped the cork and poured the champagne. I made eye contact with the manager on the other side of the room, and he gave me thumbs-up. I raised my glass in gratitude and then prepared to order.

"Ready to order now, or do you need more time?" the waiter asked.

"Bring your best appetizer, please," I said.

"Yes, sir," the waiter said as he walked away.

I focused my attention to Lisa.

"Lisa, I've been meaning to tell you how great I feel when I'm with you. I'd become so frustrated with dating that I was ready to give up on finding the woman that was meant for me. You've made my life so complete again."

She shared the same feelings. "You don't have to say it. I can tell by the way you treat me. Thank you for filling a void in my life. Will, I love you so much, it's scary."

I reached across the table and held Lisa's hand. Smiling, I looked deep into her eyes.

The waiter approached with a covered, silver serving platter. "Time for your appetizer, sir?"

I gestured to the waiter to wait a second. I stood, walked over, and knelt beside Lisa.

Still holding both her hands, I took a deep breath and said, "Lisa, I know we've only known each other a few months. But they have been heaven on earth for me. My mother always told me that when I meet the girl of my dreams, I would definitely know it. I've never been so sure of anything in my life. I would be honored if you would spend the rest of your life by my side. As my wife, my best friend, and one day, the mother of my children."

At that precise moment, I nodded to the waiter, who then removed the cover of the serving platter. There on the tray sat a miniature replica of the serving platter; inside…a sparkling one-carat diamond engagement ring. Nervous as hell, I popped the question: *"Lisa, will you marry me?"*

Lisa placed her hand over her mouth. After a moment she nodded 'yes' through her tears. I smiled and placed the ring on her finger. We both stood slowly, kissed, and embraced.

To my surprise, my marriage proposal caught the attention of the whole restaurant. Everyone applauded as the pianist began to play; *"Here Comes The Bride."*

Lisa and I were embarrassed by all the attention. We quietly seated ourselves again and prepared to order dinner. Throughout the course of the night we received several bottles of champagne from other couples, and discovered that the manager had taken care of our dinner bill. This time, I gave him the thumbs-up and he nodded, smiling.

Lisa and I prepared to leave the restaurant. As we walked toward the door, everyone in the restaurant stood and applauded again. Before exiting, Lisa and I turned to face everyone.

We took a bow, and I whispered to Lisa, "Damn, this was a helluva night. Let's do this again next week."

We drove to my apartment, passing the St. Louis Cardinals' Busch Stadium on our way to Interstate 70. As we traveled down the interstate passing the St. Louis Arch, which glistened with the reflected city lights, we tried to comprehend the magnitude of the commitment we'd just made.

We awoke the next morning in my apartment, with slight headaches from all the champagne we drank. Lisa rested her head on my chest; I kissed her forehead and ran my fingers through her hair.

"Uh-oh! It's eight o'clock. I think you definitely missed your curfew. Your father's gonna be pissed."

Lisa kissed me on the cheek and said, "Who cares? I'm getting married."

"You sure, now? This is your opportunity to change your mind."

Lisa looked at me and smiled, "Not on your life, buddy."

I gave her a kiss and said, "I will cherish and adore you every minute of every hour. Your lips will whisper my name before falling asleep at night, and in the morning when you first open your eyes."

She looked at me and smiled again, "Wowww, You're gooooodd!"

Eventually, Lisa and I dressed and headed for her house. Upon arriving, we tried to brace ourselves for the fireworks.

"Well, you ready?" Lisa asked while putting her key in the lock.

As she turned the knob, the door was yanked open by her father. The thrust of the door opening pulled Lisa inside.

"Boy, what the hell did I tell you about her curfew!" Mr. Montague roared.

I stood there speechless, too afraid to answer.

He turned and directed his anger toward Lisa, "What the hell do you think you're doing, staying out all night? What's it going to be? You moving out or what?"

Lisa hesitated before answering, "Well...yes, I'm moving out. We're getting married, Daddy."

Lisa showed the engagement ring to her father. Now it was Mr. Montague who was speechless. He glared at me as if he were trying to decide whether he should kill me slowly or get it over with quickly.

Thank God, Mrs. Montague appeared from behind the front door, holding a cordless telephone.

She emotionally embraced Lisa, "Congratulations, baby. I'm so happy for you!"

Mrs. Montague looked at the ring while Mr. Montague approached me again.

With his eyebrows knitting together in a fierce frown, he said, "So, young man from Brandon, Mississippi. You want to marry my daughter, huh?"

I could barely form a response. "Y-Y-Yes, sir. I m-m-mean, if it meets with your approval?"

Mr. Montague continued to stare at me briefly. Hesitantly, he said, "Well, you have my blessing. Welcome to the family."

"Thank you sir," I said, and we shook hands.

Mrs. Montague embraced me and kissed me on the cheek. Seeing her with that cordless phone, I couldn't resist the temptation to ask, "Mrs. Montague?"

"Yes, Will," she answered.

"Why are you holding that phone? Were you going to call the paramedics after your husband finished with me?"

My question brought about a laugh from everyone, including my future father in-law.

Mrs. Montague embraced me again. "Oh, Will! You're going to fit right in with the family."

Mr. and Mrs. Montague entered the house with Lisa and I trailing behind.

I whispered to Lisa and she smacked me on the arm as I commented, "You know, your mother still didn't answer my question about holding that phone."

Scene 14

INT—AIR TRAFFIC FACILITY—LOUISVILLE, KENTUCKY—(1990)

The first four years of marriage were wonderful. Our marriage seemed to grow stronger with each passing year. We'd been blessed with two beautiful children: Kristin, 3, and Corey, 8 months. Corey was so big that he was already the size of a one-year-old and had no problem keeping up with his sister.

During this time in our lives, I accepted a job offer from the Federal Aviation Administration. I had no idea that the decision would turn my life upside down.

What I thought when I accepted the job was, *I've finally landed the big one*. I'd always dreamed of having the ultimate career in aviation, a career as an air traffic controller with the Federal Aviation Administration. Neither the horror stories of the stress nor the high washout rate surrounding this profession didn't phase me in the least.

It was a few weeks before Christmas. I'd successfully completed the intense air traffic training at the Federal Aviation Administration's Academy in Oklahoma City. My flight from Oklahoma was scheduled to arrive around 7 p.m. in St. Louis. I hadn't seen Lisa and the kids in much too long, and I eagerly anticipated my reunion with them.

The plane finally touched down from a flight that seemed to last forever. I exited the arrival gate and immediately started searching for Lisa and the kids as I walked down the concourse.

I heard her yell my name and as I looked farther down the concourse, I saw Lisa running toward me with that beautiful smile. She always seemed to light up the day for me wherever we were, and this was even more true that day. Kristin was running as fast as she could behind her, desperately trying to keep up. Corey sat in his stroller, holding on for dear life, with his bottle dangling between his teeth. When Lisa reached me, I lifted her and whirled her around. She was breathless from running down the concourse.

"Put me down, stupid, so I can catch my breath," she said between gasps.

I let her down and kissed and kissed her while holding her close. I greeted Kristin, who was now blushing after watching Mommy and I kissing. I lifted her in my arms, giving her a big hug and a kiss. Kristin had changed so much during the time I was at the Academy, and she was becoming more beautiful by the day.

While drinking his bottle of juice, Corey sat in his stroller taking in all the excitement. He was now slightly more than a year old and seemed to struggle to remember me.

As he stared at me, his eyes seem to say, *"Man, I know this dude from somewhere."*

Lisa laughed and said, "Corey's just waking up from a short nap. He's probably a little disoriented."

"Being pushed down the concourse like he was in the Indianapolis 500 probably doesn't help either," I said, smiling.

I knelt in front of Corey's stroller to give him a better look at Dad, hoping it would refresh his memory. Corey took the empty juice bottle that was dangling between his teeth and flung it at me, striking me square on the nose.

"Ouch," I said as I looked at Lisa, "What's that about?"

Lisa turned to face Kristin, and Kristin looked down at the floor, partially embarrassed.

"A new trick he learned from big sister!" Lisa explained.

I smiled and winked at Kristin, "Heyyy..good one, Kris!"

I stood and lifted Corey in my arms. I kissed him on the cheek, smiled, and said, "Hello, Baby Buddha," the nickname that I'd given him when he was six months old.

Hearing that name brought a big smile to his face, which showed the few teeth he possessed, and he said, "Daadddy."

We reached the car in the parking lot and Lisa suggested, "You'd better let me drive, because somebody has a lot to update you on," as she pointed at Kristin.

On the ride home, Lisa and I had a million questions for each other, but our conversation was temporarily put on hold. Kristin had plenty of pictures and letters that she had saved for me, while Corey chimed in on occasion with his own version of what he had been doing. Kristin was deemed Corey's interpreter by default, due to the fact that she was the only one who could understand him. So, as Corey babbled, Lisa and I desperately looked to Kristin to interpret what he was saying.

We spent the weekend with Lisa's parents while making preparations to leave for Louisville, Kentucky; the city where I would begin my new air traffic career. I didn't have very much time to waste before reporting, so the following Monday, I loaded up the moving van that we'd rented, and we were off.

Lisa and I were excited about beginning life in a new city, and we couldn't wait to get there.

While I was concentrating on completing training at the FAA Academy, Lisa had taken care of selling our home in St. Louis. Also, with the help of her parents, she'd located a lovely two-storey home in a sought-after area in Louisville that was widely known for its outstanding schools. Even though I had only seen pictures of the house, we closed the deal. I trusted Lisa's judgment and taste. Besides, coming from the small house that I grew up in, pleasing me didn't take much.

As we traveled east on interstate 64, I drove the moving van with Lisa trailing behind in the car. Fascinated with the size of the moving van, Kristin and Corey decided to accompany me in the cab.

The trip to Louisville took us about four hours. Kristin and Corey managed to keep me company for half the trip before falling asleep. We arrived at our new home in the early afternoon and began the tedious task of unloading the moving van. Purchasing the new house had depleted our savings, so hiring a relocating company was out of the question. Being new to the city, I didn't have any friends to call. So Lisa and I took a deep breath, rolled up our sleeves, and got busy!

We worked well into the early morning before unloading the last box. Because of all the excitement, Kristin and Corey were so tired that they slept through most of the process. After a hot, soothing bath, Lisa and I crashed as well.

We slept until early afternoon, when the kids awakened us. It was lunchtime and of course they were starving. Everyone dressed for the day and we decided to go out for lunch, as well as a little sightseeing.

My first impression of the city was great. Louisville, though smaller than St. Louis, is like that city located on a riverfront. My only knowledge of Louisville history was that it was home to Muhammad Ali, the Louisville Slugger baseball bat, and the Kentucky Derby.

The next day was my first official reporting day at Louisville Center. Lisa prepared a delicious breakfast of bacon, eggs, pancakes, fresh fruit, and home-fried potatoes, making sure that I started the day off right. Full of excitement and anticipation, I quickly finished breakfast. I gave her a kiss and went out the door.

It was a beautiful day and I couldn't wait to get started in my new career. I felt confident and determined not to let anything spoil the opportunity I'd waited a lifetime for.

I arrived at the facility about twenty minutes later. I parked and confidently strutted to the entrance. At the double glass doors displaying the large FAA emblem, I took a deep breath. A few steps inside, I was approached by a lanky Caucasian man.

"You must be Will Taylor?" he asked.

"Yes, I am."

"I'm Steve Schumacher, the facility manager. Welcome to Louisville Center. It's a pleasure to meet you." He extended his hand.

Accepting the handshake, I replied, "It's a pleasure to meet you too."

Steve smiled. "It's good to finally put a face with a name. I see you made it through the Academy all right."

I nodded. "Tough, but thank God I got through it. We had several that washed out."

"Well, how 'bout I show you the control room?"

"Sounds great."

Steve and I walked down the hall to the control room floor. I felt overwhelmed upon seeing the control room floor for the first time. Many controllers were on duty, communicating with pilots via headsets. Numerous weather maps and hundreds of lights and switches filled the room, illuminating every position.

Steve and I made our way around the room, greeting each controller during breaks in pilot calls. After completing our rounds, we stopped at the supervisor's desk.

"Will, this is Dennis Cummings, the supervisor on duty," Steve said.

I extended my hand to greet Dennis. To my surprise, instead of shaking my hand, he handed me what looked liked a small white paper sack.

Puzzled, I asked, "What's this?"

"Barf bag! I bet you'll need it before the week is over," Dennis said with a mischievous smile.

The room full of controllers responded in laughter after listening to Dennis' comments. Feeling the excitement and electricity of the other controller's laughter, Dennis turned to face them and lifted both arms in the air.

Using the mannerisms of a Southern Baptist preacher, he began a short speech, "Hey, listen up…I would like to announce that a black man is in the facility! Louisville Approach is now officially integrated!"

All the controllers applauded Dennis' brief sermon. I, however, failed to see the humor. My cheekbones tightened and my nostrils flared. I gave Dennis a stare cold enough to almost pierce his skin. The room became quiet. I approached Dennis, stopping only a few inches from his face.

Unsure of what I might do, Dennis commented, "Careful, black man, take a look around. None a yo' St. Louis brothas here to watch yo' back!"

I stood firm. "They're all my brothers…Air Traffic Controllers like me, except for one redneck cracker flapping his lips, overcompensating for an obvious lack of ability!"

I wanted to beat this guy senseless. But I suddenly realized that this whole stint had been engineered to test my reaction to a little adversity.

Calming down, I handed the barf bag back to Dennis and said, "And for the record, I'm originally from a small town down South. Down there, we use rednecks for target practice!"

We glared at one another, trying to stare the other down until Steve stepped in between us. "Okay, you guys, that's it! My office. Now. Both of ya!"

Dennis and I followed Steve out of the control room.

"You know, my last trainee couldn't handle the pressure. I washed him out in six weeks. I think you're gonna do just fine, Will," Dennis said as he extended his hand toward me.

"Damn! My first day on the job and you got me in the manager's office already," I said to Dennis as I hesitantly shook his hand.

"Don't worry about it," Dennis assured me. "I'm in Steve's office all the time."

Dennis smiled, and I allowed a slow smile to come to my face in return, all the time wondering, *What tha hell have I gotten myself into?"*

Scene 15

INT—AIR TRAFFIC FACILITY—CERTIFICATION

Lisa and the kids were in the kitchen unpacking boxes. I greeted them with a kiss and said to Lisa, "Hi, babe, how are ya?"

"Hey, how was your first day?" she asked eagerly.

I smiled and tried to mask my true feelings when I replied, "Well, let's just say it was pretty interesting."

I dared not tell Lisa about the day's festivities. I didn't want her wondering whether we had indeed made the right decision in moving to Louisville.

Kristin and Corey discovered a box of toys as they unpacked, and they tromped off to play in the family room. Lisa and I continued our conversation about my first day while placing dishes in the cupboard.

"So, Mr. Air Traffic Controller, what do you think of the facility?"

I sighed before answering, "The manager, Steve, seemed pretty nice. But I can tell you one thing that I didn't see."

"What's that?"

I wiped a few drops of perspiration from my forehead and paused briefly. "There aren't any black people."

Lisa abruptly stopped her unpacking to give me her complete attention. Placing both hands on her hips, she asked, "You sure? I mean....it's only your first day."

"Oh, I'm sure babe -- especially after the conversation I had with one of the controllers today."

Afraid that I might have made her a little uneasy, I smiled and said, "Don't sweat it; I've been in this situation many times before."

After a momentary silence, we resumed our unpacking. I discovered two of the kids' plastic water pistols in the bottom of a box.

"Hey, how'd those get in there?" I muttered to myself.

Lisa continued to open boxes, too preoccupied to notice as I filled up the water pistols with tap water. I sprayed her with both weapons. She screamed and started to run down the hall.

"Stop it, Will! You're getting me all wet! You're making a mess all over the house!"

I chased Lisa around the house, both of us laughing. Kristin and Corey loved it and I began to squirt them, too.

"What are you li'l munchkins laughing at? I got something for you, too!"

I chased Kristin and Corey around the house as well, until Lisa attacked from the rear. She jumped on my back and wrestled me to the floor. Kristin and Corey came to her aid, and all of a sudden, it was dog pile on Dad time.

It was truly a wonderful time in our lives, and we had no trouble adapting to our new lifestyle. My first year on the job consisted mostly of training. I spent countless hours learning FAA rules and regulations, as well as controlling aircraft on position with training instructors.

With each day, my confidence grew and I progressed with training ahead of schedule. During that time, some controllers remained distant. However, I certainly gained the respect of most on the day of my certification.

There were major thunderstorms in the area that day, and working traffic was nearly impossible. It was a horrible day for a certification evaluation, but there was no way I was going to chicken out and let the other controllers think I couldn't cut it.

Numerous aircraft were in a holding pattern, landing one at a time because of the hail, lightning, and -- a pilot's worst nightmare -- LLWS (low-level wind shear) in the area.

The controller at the neighboring position was having a hard time concentrating because of the intense stress, and I found myself giving him support. This made the pilot nervous as hell.

"Louisville Approach, this is American two one niner heavy. How much longer you gonna keep us in this holding pattern?"

The controller responded, "American two one niner heavy, Louisville Approach, the thunderstorm is directly overhead, and we have wind gust up to five zero knots, sir."

Unfortunately, his answer was not what the pilot wanted to hear.

"Well...I'm running on fumes up here, so I'm afraid I have no choice. American two one niner heavy declaring a minimum fuel emergency...I'm starting my descent."

The controller nervously responded, "Two one niner heavy, roger min. fuel emergency...we'll clear a path for you."

"No! Look!" I shouted as I pointed to the thunderstorm on the radar, "Level six, and it's sittin right on top of us. The wind shear will rip him to pieces."

"He declared min. fuel, Will," the controller said.

The pilot was flying by the seat of his pants. "Approach, two one niner heavy, we're now about twenty miles out....very limited visibility, experiencing severe turbulence."

I keyed my headset and acknowledged, "Roger, two one niner heavy."

I turned to the other controller, unkeyed my headset and shouted, "Get the crash unit rolling right now!"

I keyed my headset again quickly and gave the pilot descent instructions: "Two one niner heavy, no other traffic a factor, sir....descend at your discretion."

Dennis, the supervisor on duty, came over to lend a hand. "What you got, Will?"

I updated Dennis as quickly as I could, "American two one niner heavy, no fuel. Thunderstorm moving northeast, wind zero four zero at three zero, gusts up to six zero. Golf-ball size hail."

Dennis unkeyed, "Damn it, the wind shear sensors are goin' crazy, they can't land in this -- you're gonna have crispy critters all over the runway."

"Approach, two one niner heavy...lightning strike! Lost some instruments and on-board radar...experiencing extreme turbulence, just dropped a thousand feet," the pilot said frantically.

"Crap, he's toast. How's he gonna navigate through the storm?" Dennis asked while shaking his head.

I turned to face Dennis. "We'll have to do it for him."

"No way, Bubba...That's a solid wall of thunderstorms!"

I leaned over toward Dennis, stopping a few inches from his face.

"How do you wanna kill them, getting through the storm or running out of gas?" I said quietly.

I focused my attention to the radar, sizing up the magnitude of the thunderstorm.

I pointed to the screen and then said to Dennis, "There! There's a small break about thirty degrees to his right."

"Where? Don't see it, man!" Dennis said.

"It's there -- just tell him, damn it!" I said forcefully.

Dennis hesitated, all the while staring at me, "For God's sake, I hope you're right!"

Dennis keyed his headset. "American two one niner heavy, we're going to get you through the storm, sir."

The pilot responded in desperation, "Approach -- that line of thunderstorms looks solid. I haven't seen any breaks for the last fifteen miles."

Dennis unkeyed and shouted, "Come on, Will...Gimme a heading!"

"Turn him right, to zero seven zero, Dennis."

Dennis keyed up quickly, "American two one niner heavy, turn right, heading zero seven zero."

The pilot acknowledged, "Two one niner heavy turning right, zero seven zero."

Dennis unkeyed and crossed his fingers, "Come on...be there!"

The pilot secured the heading, "Two one niner heavy, heading zero seven zero."

I echoed Dennis' thoughts, "It's gotta be there!"

"Two one niner heavy, is airport in sight?" I asked the distraught pilot.

"Thunderstorm is right over the airport. He'll never be able to land. Not enough fuel left for a missed approach, won't make it back to the airport," Dennis said as he rubbed his hand across his face.

The pilot broke his momentary silence, "Negative, visibility still limited. Being bombarded by very large hailstones, and being thrown around like a cowboy at a rodeo. Having trouble…wait…wait a minute, airport in sight!"

Those were the three words that Dennis and I so badly wanted to hear.

"Two one niner heavy, wind zero five zero at three five gust five five, altimeter two niner eight five. Good luck, sir," Dennis said before unkeying.

I switched the pilot over to the control tower for landing instructions. "American two one niner heavy, try and sit her down. Contact tower, frequency one two six point four five."

All the controllers monitored the control tower's frequency, awaiting the outcome.

It was like music to our ears when we heard, "American two one niner heavy on the ground safely. This was a scary one. Good work, guys."

All the controllers cheered and took turns congratulating Dennis and myself. After looking at each other for a moment, Dennis and I shared a laugh and gave each other the high five.

I received my official certification that day with flying colors. From that day on, no one ever doubted my air traffic control qualifications again.

That night also started the beginning of a long, trusting relationship with Dennis, which was often hard to explain. There were still times that we were at each other's throat, but in times of desperate need, we knew we could always depend on each other.

Scene 16

INT—WILL AND LISA'S HOME—BEDROOM

I gave Lisa a call and gave her the news.

"Hi, babe. I'll be home soon and I'm looking forward to spending some quality time with you."

"Oh, really," she said nonchalantly.

"Thought you might wanna help me celebrate my certification as an official, licensed, air traffic controller."

I thought she was going to faint from the surprise. "What! You got your certification?"

"Yep. I'll be home soon."

Lisa was overcome. "I'm so happy for you! You've been trying so hard. I'll be ready and waiting when you get home, if you know what I mean."

"Girl, sounds like you're up to no good. And I like it!"

On the way home, I picked up a dozen roses and a bottle of champagne. I entered the house from the garage, carrying the bottle of champagne in one hand and the bouquet of roses in the other. As I walked down the hallway toward the family room, I could hear soft music in the background. I entered the family room and found it lighted only by candles. Lisa sat on the sofa. She wore black lace lingerie. She looked as if she had just stepped off the cover of a Victoria's Secret catalogue. She was truly beautiful.

"See, I knew you were up to no good," I said, smiling.

With mischievous smile, she answered, "Great timing, Mr. Taylor. I just put the kids to bed for the night."

We kissed and I gave her the bouquet of roses. "Here, babe, these are for you."

"Thanks, they're beautiful. I'll put them in water."

Lisa carried the roses to the kitchen and placed them in a vase. She returned with two champagne glasses and joined me on the sofa. I popped the cork on the bottle and filled both glasses.

Lisa smiled and congratulated me, "So, I guess congratulations are in order, Mr. Air Traffic Controller."

"There's no way that I could have done it without you. Thanks for being there every step of the way."

After a few moments, I murmured, "What do you say we take this party upstairs?"

Lisa gave me a kiss and smiled, "You just read my mind."

I lifted her in my arms and we kissed as I carried her up the stairs to our bedroom. Placing her gently on the bed, I turned off the lights, undressed as fast as I could, and joined her under the covers. We were kissing passionately when Lisa suddenly pulled away. "Will, wait a minute. Somebody's knocking on the door!"

"Huh? I didn't hear anything."

Lisa pushed me aside, "Stop it, now! Wait a minute, listen!"

There was a knock on the bedroom door and this time I heard it. I sighed as I put on my boxers and turned on the lights. I opened the bedroom door slowly and there stood Corey, the "Baby Buddha." Corey just stood there rubbing his eyes, with his empty bottle dangling between his front teeth.

"What's the problem, li'l man? You have a nightmare?"

Corey didn't answer. He continued to rub his eyes and then took the empty bottle from between his teeth and tossed it at me, hitting me square on the nose.

"Ouch!" I said, as Lisa began to laugh, "Well, damn! I guess that means he wants more juice."

Lisa stretched her arms in Corey's direction and he walked over, climbing into bed beside her. Placing both hands on my hips, I shook my head in disappointment. I picked up the empty bottle and headed downstairs to the kitchen for more juice. Needless to say, Lisa and I had the pleasure of Corey's company for the rest of the night.

As the next several years passed, Lisa and I reaped the benefits of well-paying jobs. Lisa had started a daycare business that was very profitable, and we were living a story-book, middle class lifestyle.

Kristin was now in her third year of school and continued to do exceptionally well. Her outstanding work during the previous two years had given her quite a reputation, and all the teachers in the school knew her.

Corey, now finally in kindergarten, was off to a great start as well. He was also reading beyond his current grade level and was progressing ahead of schedule. I could no longer call him "Baby Buddha." Slim and trim, he was turning into a handsome young man. Corey looked just like his mother, and the girls in his class were already chasing him at recess. Kristin often teased him when he came home with notes from girls that were left in his backpack. Corey, in turn, would tease Kristin about a certain boy in her class, and such exchanges usually ended in a shouting match. Lisa would put an end to all the shouting while I just laughed and marveled at how fast they were growing up.

To this day, I can say that I've kept my promise to myself, to never hit or exhibit abusive behavior toward my kids. I will always remember how my father hit James and me on a regular basis, and it's probably the main reason that we don't have a close relationship with our father today.

Lisa and I have always made time for our kids and shown them plenty of love. When the need arose, we've used alternative discipline techniques. I can honestly say that we have two of the most well-mannered kids on earth and the need for discipline doesn't arise often. The frequent compliments we receive from people assures us that we are indeed raising them the right way.

Our lifestyle was perfect -- almost too perfect. I felt as though our life was truly a major blessing from God himself; perhaps compensation for such a miserable childhood.

My mother often said, "Will, with each major blessing, there also comes a major storm!"

Little did I realize how major the storm would be that would turn my life upside down.

EXT—BACKYARD OF WILL AND LISA'S HOME— (1995)

I tossed a couple of steaks on the grill as I stood on the patio talking with Dennis. I had invited Dennis and his girlfriend Amy over for a backyard barbecue, and everyone seemed to be enjoying themselves. Lisa and Amy tried their hand at badminton in the backyard with Kristin and Corey but proved to be no competition for the kids.

"Thanks for havin' me and Amy over today, man. I appreciate it," Dennis said.

"Glad you guys could make it. You definitely have a cute one there."

"I dunno, Will. Maybe I should settle down like you."

"Maybe it's time to stop landing planes and find a new business, or something less stressful," I said, somewhat agreeing with Dennis.

"You can't leave! You're the quota! Don't leave me alone with all those white guys!" Dennis responded in his usual, bad-sense-of-humor way.

"That's getting to be less and less funny, Dennis!"

"All right, I'll be less funny. It has crossed my mind....is it important to have more blacks there? Honestly?"

"Yeah. It's time. If you don't take steps, the door will always be closed."

Dennis grabbed another beer from the cooler, popping the top before responding, "I thought it was all about who is best for the job, not givin' a position to a less-qualified minority."

"It is, but unless you have a level playing field, you can never find out who is best."

This conversation was nothing new to us; we had discussed the topic before on a number of occasions. As always, the result was a heated discussion.

"Don't give me that equal-opportunity/affirmative-action crap, Will! Lives are at stake here! Affirmative action is preferential treatment -- the only ones who benefit are minorities and women.

"I think you have a misconception of affirmative action! A person still has to be qualified for a position. It just gives minorities and women a fair chance!"

"Here's an idea," Dennis said. "Why not treat everyone equally and judge them by merit!"

"Sounds good to me, Dennis, but I think someone forgot to tell the agency because 98 percent of the top jobs are held by white males."

Kristin interrupted our discussion, tugging on my shirt and saying, "Daddy...Daddy, telephone. It's Grandpa in Mississippi."

I shoved the cooking utensils at Dennis, relinquishing the rights to the grill. I stepped through the sliding glass patio door and into the kitchen for a little privacy.

"Hello," I said.

"That you, Will?" the voice responded.

"Hi Dad," I answered.

"How ya doin', fly boy? I ain't heard from you in a coon's age!"

My father always had a unique ensemble of words and you never knew what he might say next. He had rarely called, and when he did, some sort of ulterior motive usually revealed itself.

"Got some friends over for a li'l barbecue. What you want?"

"Well, I hate to ruin yo' barbecue, baby boy. I'm 'fraid I'm at County Hospital with yo' Mama."

He had my full attention. "What! What you do to her?"

"Wait a minute now, boss man, just calm down. She was havin' chest pains earlier, but she doin' much betta now. They released her from 'tensive care and put her in another room. She sleep and just restin'."

I was furious but still very concerned. "When did this happen?"

"You can thank yo' brother James. This time he almost killed her."

My father sighed before giving me the details. "Showed up on the doorstep 'bout two this morning after one his crack binges. Somebody pistol-whipped his sorry ass good."

This news made me sad for James, but I was more concerned for my mother.

"How long they gonna keep her there?"

"Doctor said fa' couple days. Ain't got much trust, though, in that doctor. Hell, his li'l ass 'bout the same age you."

I took a moment to regain my senses from the shock of all the news.

"When Mama wakes up, you tell her I'm on the way."

I slammed the phone down on the counter. "Damn it!" I shouted.

Lisa heard the noise and came running in from the patio. "What's wrong, babe?" she asked. I hesitantly gave her the details.

It was 1995, and things had really gone downhill for my brother James. He had graduated from marijuana to crack cocaine. Often, after using all his money to purchase drugs, he would trade his car as payment for more. His life had been spiraling steadily downward for a long time. But this time, the effect on my mother was the worst it had ever been.

I was devastated by the news. After saying goodbye to Lisa and the kids, I drove to Mississippi with my heart in my throat.

I walked down the hallway in the hospital, frantically searching for my mother's room. I stopped at the nurse's station to ask which room my mother occupied. The nurse pointed to the adjacent room. Before opening the door, I paused, trying to regain my composure. I opened the door slowly and there lay my mother, asleep. I stood there, momentarily stunned by the tubes, monitors, and other equipment that held her captive. I walked over, sat on the bed beside her, and gathered her hand in mine.

"Mama…Mama, can you hear me? It's Will."

She slowly opened her eyes, and I kissed her on the forehead.

She forced a tired smile, saying, "Boy, what in tha world you doing here? I almost didn't know who you was. Stand up, let Mama look at you."

I was happy to comply.

"My, my, my. Look at my baby. Mr. Air Traffic Controller himself. All dressed up in yo' 'spensive suit. I'm so proud of you, baby. Hey, where Lisa and my grandbabies?"

I sat on the bed again and took a few photographs from the inside pocket of my jacket.

"Here, Mama, they sent pictures for you."

"Well, I declare. They sho are some beautiful kids."

"How you feelin', Mama?"

"Doctor said I can probably go home tomorrow. Said I should just take it easy for a while, try and relieve as much stress as possible. That's why I sent yo' father to work this mornin'," she said, and we both shared a laugh.

"Hope you plan on making some changes. You know, stop worrying so much," I said.

"That's what I wanted to talk to you about."

"What's on your mind?" I eagerly asked.

"James been in and out of drug rehab, and still can't leave that crack alone. Last time him and yo' father got into it, yo' father pulled out his gun. I know it's just a matta of time before somebody ends up dead."

"Yeah, I know. This time it was almost you."

My mother grabbed my arm and, with my help, pulled herself up to a sitting position.

"Will, you the only one left I can turn to. I ain't neva' asked you fa' nothin', but this time I'm askin' you....let James come live wit you."

I looked down at the floor, shaking my head as I sighed, "Mama, no! You know I can't do that."

My mother pleaded her case. "James won't listen to nobody else but you. He just need a change in his life right now and you the only one that can help him start off in the right direction!"

"Mama, you don't understand. James has been smoking crack for the last few years. Once you get hooked on crack, you might as well be dead!"

Infuriated by my comment, my mother slapped me across the face.

"Don't you say that 'bout yo' brother! James is still 'live! He the same brother that saved you from gettin' run over by them

84

Klan rednecks. He the same brother looked out for you all the time when you was growing up. Now it's yo' time to look out fa' him!"

Scene 18

EXT—WILL'S CAR—HIGHWAY

As James and I traveled down the highway back to Louisville, we were mostly silent. The tension was thick enough for a scythe. I had a thousand thoughts racing through my mind, searching desperately for a solution to the situation. But most of all, I didn't know how Lisa would react to having James as a new house guest.

My brother was first to break the silence. "I really 'preciate you lettin' me stay with you fa' a while, li'l brother."

I turned the radio down and looked at James with an angry stare. "What did you say? Man, I can't believe you, James. Don't thank me for anything. The only reason I'm doing this is for Mama…not for your sorry ass. Are you even aware of what you been doing to her? What you been puttin' her through?"

"I know I been screwing up, but you don't understand, man. I can't seem to catch a break."

As usual, James tried to put the blame on someone or something other than himself.

But, as always, I wasn't buying it. "You can't catch a break because all you think about is gettin' high. You're caught up in all the sex and drugs in that crack world and you don't want to let it go. You're gonna keep using until you end up in jail or you're lying somewhere with a bullet hole in your forehead."

James looked at me with an expression of discontent and then reclined his seat.

With his eyes closed, he said, "All these years, and you still trying to preach to yo' big brother."

Rubbing my left hand across the back of my neck, I responded, "Yeah, and I still don't know why."

We both remained quiet for the next few hours until arriving in Louisville. It wasn't long before I turned into the subdivision and pulled into the garage.

James couldn't resist commenting, "Damn, Will! This yo' house? Looks like you doin' all right for a small-town country boy."

I ignored James' comment and unloaded the luggage. I handed James his suitcase and forcefully grabbed his arm.

"A few words of advice before we go inside. This whole situation about you living here is totally new to Lisa. So you make sure you're on your best behavior."

"I hear ya', baby boy....Now let go my arm. Damn!" he said as he pulled away.

James and I entered the house carrying our luggage. Immediately, Kristin and Corey greeted me.

"All right, Daddy's home!" Kristin said.

I knelt to give her and Corey a hug. "Hey, you li'l munchkins. How ya'll doing?"

Kristin and Corey had seen James on only a few occasions, but he always had a way of making a favorable impression on them. I guess you could say that he was the "cool" uncle or relative that many people have in their family. Kristin was the most fond of James.

Kristin wasted no time in asking, "Daddy, you brought Uncle James?"

"Yep. Gonna stay with us for a while. Say hello."

Kristin and Corey ran over to greet James. James lifted them both in the air, giving them a hug.

"Hey, how's my favorite niece and nephew doing?"

"Fine," Kristin said, "We're your only niece and nephew, remember?" Kristin said with the quick wit that she inherited from her mother.

James laughed and kissed Kristin on the cheek. "Oh yeah, I keep forgetting that."

Lisa stood at the end of the hallway with her arms folded. The look on her face was as cold as ice. I walked over and gave her a kiss on the cheek. Her arms remained folded and she didn't crack a smile.

"Hi, babe," I said, as she continued to glare at me, "It's only for a little while."

Lisa walked toward James and the kids without a sound.

"Kris, Corey, give Daddy a hug goodnight, it's bedtime! You have school tomorrow," she said.

The kids' reply was the same as every night at bedtime. "Aw, Mom, do we have to?"

"Go ahead now, it's getting late."

Kristin and Corey ran over to me and I gave them a hug.

Hoping to delay bedtime, Kristin asked, "Did you bring us anything from Mississippi?"

"Yeah, did you?" Corey echoed.

Corey was young, but he was learning the ropes quickly, thanks to Kris.

"Yep. It's in my suitcase. Let's go upstairs and I'll show ya."

I grabbed my suitcase and headed upstairs with the kids. I unpacked the kids' present and sent them to their room. I eased my way to the top of the stairs and found myself eavesdropping on Lisa and James' conversation.

Lisa approached James, shaking her head in disappointment.

James was the first to say something. "Sister-in-law, how ya doin'? Long time no see."

"Hello, James," Lisa answered.

"Now that I'm wit my li'l brother and his family, I'm ready fa' a new start."

Lisa wasn't buying it. "Uh-huh. I guess we'll see. Let's get one thing straight right now. You know I've always been able to see right through your bull. Will and I have built a wonderful life, and I won't let anybody screw it up. The last thing I want to see is you letting him down, and for him to regret that he brought you here!"

"Whoa now, I hear what ya sayin. He my baby brother and I been lovin' him a lot longa than you. The last thang I want to do is hurt Will or harm yo' family. It ain't like that and I'm gon' prove it to you."

Lisa folded her arms again, but hesitated before responding. "Yeah, right! Grab your bags, I'll show you to the guest bedroom."

Later that night, as Lisa and I lay in bed, Lisa turned her back to me as we discussed the situation.

"I know you're mad at me, Lisa, and I'm sorry. I know I should've discussed it with you first."

Lisa angrily turned over to face me before answering, "Will, what on earth were you thinking? Did you even consider me and the kids? Did you consider the valuables in the house? What is it that you think you can do for him now?"

I desperately tried to plead my case. "I understand what you're saying. If I thought that he was truly a danger to you and the kids, I would have never brought him here. I'm going to try and get him back into rehab."

It seemed that Lisa had already made her mind up about James. "Once a crack head, always a crack head!"

I, however, wasn't quite ready to give up on family. If James had one ounce of hope left in him, I felt as though I owed my mother at least that much.

"I promised Mama. When I saw her lying there in that hospital bed, aged and helpless, I knew I had to do something. Please, please, just try and understand that I had to."

INT—AIR TRAFFIC FACILITY

I returned to work a few days later. Things had been tense around the house and I was glad to use work as an escape outlet. This particular morning I worked on position beside Dennis, carrying on conversations between pilot calls.

Steve, the facility manager, entered the control room escorting a man who appeared to be a new hire. He made his way around the room in the company of Steve, shaking hands with each controller. Dennis and I observed from our positions.

"I thought the next hire was going to be a minority," I said to Dennis.

"It was. Luther…" Dennis said as he looked at me and smiled.

I couldn't believe it. "They're counting the janitor in their diversity hiring?"

"Like I told you before Will, we already have our facility quota."

During the facility meetings in the past few years, minority recruitment had always been one of the topics that were discussed.

I had consistently made it a point to voice my opinion, but it was always the same story from Steve: "We're still searching for qualified candidates, and hopefully the next one will be a minority."

Steve and the new hire finally made it over to Dennis and I.

Steve introduced him. "Dennis, Will, meet Doug Armstrong. A new controller."

We shook hands, and Dennis rested his arm on my shoulder.

"Doug, I'm Dennis Cummings and this is Will Taylor."

"We're twins," I said.

Dennis jokingly played along. "I guess you can say I'm the black sheep of the family."

Doug was caught off guard and didn't know whether he should smile or take offense. Steve, on the other hand, failed to see the humor.

I seized the opportunity to take a shot at Steve. "Well, I can see that all the talk about minority recruitment was just lip service."

Steve glared at me but refused the confrontation. He turned and walked away, with Doug following behind like a lost puppy.

"Careful, black man, don't want to get a reputation of being uppity," Dennis said as he patted me on the back.

Dennis and I turned our chairs around to face our control positions. He asked, "Where you been the last couple of days, man?"

"None of your business," I said jokingly.

"I hope that all the li'l black kids got to watch the Million Man March," Dennis said in an off the wall comment.

"Yeah, that was a great sign of unity," I agreed.

"Right, but they could also see what their fathers look like for the first time!"

As I suspected, Dennis had set me up for one of his bad-sense-of-humor jokes. But in light of all the new occurrences that were happening in my life, I wasn't up to a sparring round with him.

"That's cute," I said, hoping he would take the hint and chill.

Unfortunately, it didn't work. "Did you hear bout the million black men who went to Washington?" he asked.

"Enough, Dennis!" I said firmly, but to no avail.

"It turns out that only five of them missed work, and you were one of them."

Dennis pushed too far and finally got the confrontation he wanted.

"You got somethin' to get off your chest, Dennis?"

"Word is, you skipped out on us to march with your brothers."

"Word is wrong. You were there. I went to see my mother."

Dennis looked indecisive. "I don't know where you went. The guys want to know who you are. You an air traffic controller or a black air traffic controller?"

Dennis was trying to push my buttons and he had succeeded, almost to the point of bodily harm. I abruptly stood and walked over to Dennis' position, stopping a few inches from his face.

At that precise moment, he received a hit from a pilot calling up on frequency, "Approach, Delta three four niner heavy!"

Dennis could see how infuriated I was and was definitely glad the pilot had saved his ass. "Hold on, Will, I got a bite!"

I stood there glaring at Dennis momentarily, then I received an aircraft calling on frequency as well. I returned to my control position and, needless to say, Dennis didn't utter a single sound in my direction for the rest of shift.

After a long and frustrating afternoon at work, I arrived home that night and headed upstairs. I entered the bedroom and found Lisa lying on the bed, beautifully dressed in sexy lingerie. Soft music played in the background and several candles provided the only light. The aromatic scent of the candles was refreshing, and I immediately started to unwind.

I smiled and said to Lisa, "Well, now. Who is this strange lady in my bed?"

Lisa tried out a Swedish accent. "I am Inga, your new nanny. I am from the West side of Sweden. Your wife couldn't be here, Mr. Taylor -- she's out celebrating her wedding anniversary. So I put Kristin and Corey to sleep and slipped into my party gown."

"Wonderful," I said, "I was getting a little tired of her anyway."

Lisa gave me a sarcastic smirk, and I kissed her hand before saying, "Happy anniversary, babe."

I sat on the edge of the bed and took off my shoes. I sighed and then lay down beside Lisa.

"What's the matter? Something on your mind?" she inquired.

"Just thinkin' about something Dennis said at work today. They're not interested in hiring any more blacks because they have their quota."

"Will, you know how Dennis is. I'm sure that's not true," she said.

"I don't know anymore. It's been five years and they haven't done it yet."

"Does it bother you that you're the only one?"

I took a moment to ponder Lisa's question before answering, "Yeah...no...I guess not. I don't care if the people are Martians, just as long as the planes land safely."

93

Lisa rolled over and straddled me.

She smiled as she said, "Well, you can be my li'l Mandingo air traffic controller any time. Let's see if you can get your plane ready for takeoff.

She kissed me and began to undress me slowly. Just when things started to get interesting, we heard a knock at the door. Lisa looked at me and sighed as she rolled over. I got up and opened the door. There stood Corey with an inquisitive look.

"Yes?" I asked.

As usual, he didn't answer. He rubbed his eyes momentarily as he walked around me, and crawled in bed beside Lisa. He grabbed the television remote and began to surf the channels. Lisa laughed and thought the whole thing was hilarious as usual.

"And just where do you think you're goin', li'l man?" I asked.

"I couldn't sleep," he said.

I wasn't surprised. Lisa kissed him on the cheek and then smiled at me.

Placing both hands on my hips, I said in a sarcastic tone, "It's good to see that someone is getting somethin' tonight, even if it is just a little attention."

I turned to exit the room. "Where ya goin', Dad?" Corey asked.

"To take a cold shower, li'l man."

Corey turned to Lisa and asked, "Mom, why does Dad like taking cold showers?"

It was typical of how the day had gone and, after taking a shower, I was ready to crash. By now, Lisa and Corey were both asleep and I couldn't wait to join them. It had been a long day. Exhausted, I was asleep before my head hit the pillow.

I slept for a few hours until I was awakened by loud music, blaring downstairs.

"God, what now?" I thought as I jumped out of bed and stormed downstairs.

It was two o'clock in the morning and James sat in the family room with a six-pack of beer, blasting the stereo.

"Hey, baby bro. You want ta drank a beer with yo' big brother?"

I angrily responded, "What tha hell you doing, James? You can't be drinking and blasting the stereo this late. It's two in the morning! Lisa and I have to work tomorrow, and the kids have school."

"Why you always wanna shut my party down, Will?"

"Man, turn that stereo off and take yo' ass to bed. I keep tellin' you, life ain't one big party."

I turned the stereo off and stormed back upstairs. I returned to bed and glanced over at Lisa, hoping she wasn't awakened by all the excitement downstairs. No such luck. Lisa looked at me with an expression of anger and then turned her back to me without saying a word.

The next several months proved to be quite trying. James mostly worked afternoon jobs and after work, he would come home with a case of beer, "to unwind," as he called it. I allowed James some latitude and even purchased headphones for the stereo. However, the simple task of showing him how to use them was like teaching physics to an elementary student. The result was always the same; I would have to get up in the middle of the night and turn the stereo off as a result of him being incapacitated from alcohol.

James' irresponsibility, along with his consistent alcohol abuse, led to his inability to maintain employment. Even though he was terminated from several jobs, it didn't seem to phase him one bit.

Lisa had never been through a situation such as this and constantly kept her guard up. She remained skeptical; taking precautions such as hiding her jewelry and locking bedroom doors whenever she left the house. In order to try to keep the peace, I remained silent, acting as though I didn't notice her behavior.

I definitely knew that James was an alcoholic and a cocaine addict, but I had always felt in my heart that he would never steal anything from me or my family. I guess it was that brotherly bond from growing up together in such adverse conditions. If there's one positive thing I can say about the whole predicament, it's that James has never proven me wrong when it comes to thievery. For that reason, I wasn't quite ready to give up on him.

I found myself frantically searching for a solution to my brother's chemical dependency.

I wanted desperately to please my mother. It was as if I were the last hope for James.

I wanted to prove myself at work. The whole facility had turned its back on me, for whatever reason, since the *Million Man March.*

Most of all, the whole situation was beginning to weigh heavily on my marriage. I wondered how much more of this storm I could bear. However, this storm was just beginning, and I had no idea how intense it would become.

Scene 20

INT—WILL AND LISA'S HOME—FAMILY ROOM

It was becoming impossible to keep the peace at home. After a long and restless night, I arrived at work that morning only to find an unannounced facility meeting in session. Steve was in charge and, as I approached, he appeared to be speaking his mind about minority recruitment. I entered the room and pulled up a chair.

Becoming aware of my presence, Steve terminated the meeting abruptly. "All agreed? Good. That's all I have."

The meeting adjourned, and I hurried to catch up with Dennis as people returned to their work stations.

"What was that all about?" I asked.

Dennis tried to blow the whole thing off. "Nothin'."

Unwilling to accept this answer, I probed further. "The entire place has a meeting and I am the only one not there? That's not 'nothin.'"

"Don't get your panties in a bunch. It was more of the usual. The new FAA lynching policy."

I grabbed Dennis' arm and firmly said, "Don't play with me today!"

Dennis looked around to see whether anyone was listening to our conversation.

"Chill, man! Just Federal edict. We have to hire more...Negroes," he looked around as if it were a secret. "And Steve didn't want any Negroes there so the Honkies could honk their minds openly."

"And?" I asked.

"I'm not gonna blow smoke up your skirt, Will, the guys love you. You're part of the family. One of the best. But none of us want the next guy hired to be black if he is not the best guy getting the planes on the ground. And I think you agree with us."

"I do. But if the best man is a black man, then the black man should be here!"

97

Dennis resumed his normal character. "Right on, brother! Now lets see the black man get Delta two one three heavy on the runway without littering the airport with passengers."

That particular day was the longest day of work in my air traffic career. Other than communicating with pilots, I didn't say a word to anyone in the facility. I felt as though I didn't have a friend in the world, or anyone who I could turn to. In the back of my mind, I knew there was always the possibility of giving FAA Headquarters in Washington a call and inform them of the situation at the facility. In doing so, I might have won the battle, but eventually, like all whistle blowers, I would have lost the war. I knew of countless horror stories of employees going against the agency and winning cases, only to have the agency retaliate in some fashion. I knew I had to keep searching for a solution but I didn't know how much more I could withstand.

I finished the workday and exited the facility quietly. With all the tension at home as well as in the facility, I assumed a new personality. I became withdrawn. My change in behavior made my co-workers more apprehensive toward me. It felt like me against the world.

I arrived home that afternoon to find James in the family room, nursing a six-pack of beer. He announced that he was getting an early start on celebrating being fired from yet another job.

After I gave James a brief lecture, he informed me that Lisa was upstairs, obviously keeping her distance because of an earlier confrontation.

I made my way upstairs. There sat Lisa in our bedroom. Other than saying hello, she continued with the cold shoulder treatment for the rest of the night. I dared not say anything to her, especially about the things that were going on at the facility.

The next morning, Lisa and I dressed the kids for school and sent them downstairs. Lisa finished dressing for work before I did and went downstairs to give them breakfast.

She was surprised to see the kids standing in the hallway, pointing in the direction of the family room.

They were laughing uncontrollably, and Lisa asked, "What's so funny?"

Kristin answered between giggles, "Uncle James is drunk! Uncle James is drunk! He fell asleep on the couch again!"

I could hear the excitement from upstairs.

Lisa instructed the kids, "Kristin and Corey, go get in the car! We'll stop for breakfast on the way. I'll be right there; I have to talk with Daddy for a minute."

I heard Lisa's footsteps as she stomped up the stairs.

As I sat on the bed tying my shoelace, I thought to myself, "Ohhh, man. Here we go again!"

The bedroom door flew open.

"Damn, baby! Why are you attacking the door?" I asked.

Lisa wasn't the least bit amused at my futile attempt at humor.

With both hands on her hips, she yelled, "That's it! I've had it! I've been patient as long as I could, but I can't take it anymore! The minute he starts to use drugs in this house, it's time for him to go!"

Trying to get Lisa to calm down, I responded, "Whoa! Wait a minute, babe, what's going on?"

"James is downstairs passed out with empty beer cans and drug stuff all over the place. The kids were downstairs laughing at him. His ass has got to go!"

"Okay, I'll talk to him, babe."

Unfortunately, that wasn't the answer Lisa was looking for.

"What? You'll talk to him. I'll tell you what…I'll make it easy for you, Will. You and James can have the house to yourselves. The kids and I are going back to St. Louis!"

Lisa slammed the bedroom door and stormed down the stairs. I hurriedly put on my other shoe and ran down the stairs after her. I followed Lisa into the garage, trying desperately to convince her to stay.

"Lisa, wait a minute. You're overreacting!"

She opened the car door and pointed in my direction. "I told you. I've had enough!"

I could tell by the look in her eyes that there was no point in trying to change her mind. The stress of the previous several months had been too much for her to handle.

I'll always remember her last words, "Will, at some time in your life you have to learn that it's okay to say no, family or not. Especially if that someone is beyond saving. Goodbye!"

Lisa got in the car and started the engine. As she backed the car out of the garage, I waved goodbye to Kristin and Corey. I stood in the garage and watched the car until it disappeared. I took a moment to regain my composure. Then I stormed inside.

James was still passed out on the sofa and with no idea of what had just transpired. I stood over him as he lay on the sofa; I looked around and took in the room. Empty beer cans littered the area. And there, on the coffee table, lay a glass crack pipe and a half-smoked joint. When I saw the drugs, my anger took over. I grabbed James and threw him off the sofa.

"JAMES, GET UP, DAMN IT!"

James took a few seconds to get his bearings. "Hey, li'l brother! What's all the shouting 'bout this morning?"

I paced back and forth. "What the hell is wrong with you, man? I told you never to bring that stuff in my house."

James began with his weak apology, "I'm sorry, Will. I meant to put it away, but I fell asleep."

"Man, you still don't get it, do you? I'm takin' you to rehab! Today!"

"I know, man. I gots to move back in wit Mama."

"No, Sir. You will not drain her anymore! Rehab or jail, your choice!"

"Come on, man. You know ain't no way. I still got some money left and if you spot me the rest, I think I can get an apartment."

"You want another handout, huh?"

James stood and approached me. "You don't think I can do it. I'll clean up this mess, get a job before the end of the day. You think you somethin' special? Give me one a' them suits and I'll prove to you I can do it."

James walked around me and into the kitchen.

"Fine. Clean, job, and out by five," I hesitantly agreed. "I have to find Lisa."

I strode down the hallway as James trailed behind with a beer he had just retrieved from the fridge.

100

"Cool! That-a-work. I think I'll drank me some breakfast. You want some?"

I turned and grabbed him by the collar.

Startled, he said nervously, "Damn, just kiddin', man!"

Scene 21

INT—AIR TRAFFIC FACILITY—(NEWSLETTER)

My search for Lisa that morning proved fruitless. I arrived at work distraught over the realization that my wife and kids were gone for good.

I entered the control room and walked over to the supervisor's desk to get a copy of the position assignments for the day. I greeted the supervisor, who was reading what appeared to be some type of memo or newsletter.

"Morning, Earl. How's it going?"

Earl didn't acknowledge my greeting and kept on reading. I assumed that he didn't hear me, so I said it again; only this time a little bit louder.

"Earl, good morning, man!"

This time, Earl looked up from reading the newsletter.

In a stern voice, he said, "Get on position!" and then continued reading the newsletter.

I stood there momentarily, glaring at Earl before speaking, "What's your problem this morning?"

Earl didn't respond and just kept on reading. Tired of being ignored, I walked to my position.

"Morning, Will," Dennis said, as I plugged my headset in.

I asked Dennis immediately, "What the hell is wrong with Earl this morning, he hung over again?"

Dennis smiled and answered, "Probably that arrogant, upstate New York attitude that comes out now and then."

"Well, I'm the last person he wants to piss off this morning!"

Dennis was concerned. "What's going on, man?"

Unsure about airing my personal laundry at work, I said hesitantly, "Trouble at home. Just trying to keep the peace with both sides of the family."

I worked on position for a few hours, but the worry about how to find Lisa weighed heavily on my mind. I decided to make a few telephone calls to try to locate her. I stretched the cord from my headset across the room to the supervisor's desk. I picked up the telephone and began dialing a few phone numbers of possible places she could be. Unfortunately, each attempt brought no news.

"Hey, get on position, traffic's building," the supervisor said.

It was my turn to ignore him, so I proceeded to make another call.

It wasn't long before Dennis chimed in, "Come on, Will, we're going down the tubes. Where's your head at today?"

"Mind your own damn business; I got a handle on my traffic," I angrily replied.

Tension began to build between Dennis and me. He responded, "Those last two jets came mighty damn close to each other!"

There was finally an answer on the phone. It was a phone call I was very reluctant to make. It was Lisa's mother.

"Hi, Mom, is Lisa there, by chance? Ahhh...no ma'am. She said earlier that she and the kids might make the trip back to St. Louis to pay you a visit. So if she comes, pretend that you're surprised."

A pilot called up on frequency, "Louisville Approach, U-P-S four one niner heavy with you level at niner thousand...."

I keyed up my headset, "U-P-S four one niner heavy, Louisville Approach, roger niner thousand."

I unkeyed quickly and said to Mrs. Montague, "Ahhh...no ma'am, nothin's wrong."

I keyed my headset again and quickly gave the pilot descent instructions. "Four one niner heavy descend and maintain seven thousand, altimeter two niner niner two."

Unkeying my headset, I ended the call, "Yes ma'am, I'm sure. Gotta go. Bye."

I was about to hang up the phone when Dennis grabbed it from my hand.

"Give me the phone, Will." He shouted into the phone, "FAA control, I need someone down here who can keep his mind on his work!"

"Don't play with me today, Dennis!" I said as I grabbed the telephone back from him and slammed it down on the desk.

The force from the telephone sent a stack of newsletters flying from the desk to the floor. Dennis and I began picking up newsletters until I glanced at the title.

It read, *THE MOUNTAINTOP*, and underneath was the subtitle, *Coalition of Federal White Aviation Employees.*

The title definitely grabbed my attention, so I continued reading the first paragraph.

Out loud, I read, "'Join the Coalition of Federal White Aviation Employees now because there is no other organization that deals with, or brings to the attention of the F. A. A., the concerns of the white male in this period of forthcoming change in personnel policies.' What the hell is this, Dennis?"

"Nothing," Dennis answered.

"Nothing? Who brought it in?" I asked.

"Hold on, I got a bite," Dennis said as we were interrupted by a pilot call.

Dennis and I returned to our positions and resumed working traffic. After the traffic spurt was over and we had a chance to catch our breath, I took a moment to glance around the room. Surprisingly, most of the controllers were reading a copy of the newsletter.

I stood, abruptly unplugged my headset from position, and marched over to the supervisor's desk.

"Earl, take over my position. I need to have a word with the manager!"

"Traffic might start to build again. What do you need to see him for?" Earl asked.

"You need a reason? Call it personal," I shouted as I walked off the control room floor.

I entered the office area and approached Mary Ann, Steve's secretary. "Steve in his office?"

"Oh…good morning, Will. Just a minute, I'll buzz him."

Mary Ann buzzed Steve on the intercom. "Will Taylor wants to see you."

Mary Ann hung up the telephone and then said, "Go on in, Will."

I knocked on Steve's door before entering. He stood and greeted me, "Hi, Will. Come on in and have a seat."

I wasted no time getting to the point. "I need to ask a question."

"Sure. What's going on?"

I handed the newsletter to Steve. "You aware of this type of literature being brought into the facility?"

Steve took a moment to look over the newsletter, then responded, "I've never seen anything like this before. Where'd you get it?"

"There are plenty of copies on the supervisor's desk. Most of the controllers took a copy, including the supervisor."

Steve asked, "Do you find it offensive?"

I slowly shook my head in disappointment before answering, "I've enjoyed working here the last five years. Mainly because this type of situation has never come up. This type of literature has no place in the FAA."

Steve seemed nonchalant. "I guess I'll look into the situation."

I didn't find Steve's answer satisfactory.

"I would like you to call Regional Headquarters and find out if that organization is being recognized or supported by the FAA."

Steve frowned, angered by the request. "I'm not calling Headquarters because I don't think it's that important. I said I'd look into the situation."

By now, Steve was out of his seat. He shouted, "I think you'd better head back to the operations floor and get back to work! NOW!"

I was totally caught off guard by Steve's attitude.

Believing that I had no other option, I sighed and stood slowly before saying, "We'll see how important Headquarters thinks it is. I'll make the call myself!"

"You go right ahead!" Steve said angrily as I exited his office.

I stormed down the hall and returned to the control room, determined to find out more details about the newsletter.

I confronted Dennis. "Have you read this newsletter?"

"Yeah, I read it, Will," he said nervously.

"Please tell me you didn't bring it in!"

My questions made Dennis uneasy. He looked around the room at the other controllers as they witnessed our conversation.

"Man, I haven't seen anything like this since I was a kid growing up in Mississippi. It's just like the literature that was being distributed by the Klan!" I said.

As always, Dennis tried to use his weak sense of humor to escape the harshness of the situation.

"It's been here for a couple of days, my li'l Muslim brother."

I had him on the ropes and I wasn't about to let up.

"No, sir, not this time. None of your jokes 'bout race…'bout quotas…'bout nothin. Straight answer, Dennis!"

"Hold on….I got a bite," he said, refusing to answer.

"This is wrong! It's all wrong! I've had it up to here! Are you going to stand with me?" I asked.

"On the black side?"

"On the right side, Dennis!"

"You know the agency always finds a way to retaliate, and I can't afford to lose this job, man," Dennis explained.

"So, it's all bull. You're just like the rest. Acting all these years as if you understood!"

"I do, but…"

"But when it comes time to stand up, you're so quick to sit down!"

The whole room remained quiet, including Steve, who had left his office to investigate all the shouting. I looked around the room, furiously glaring at all the controllers. I took my headset from around my neck and threw it across the room.

"I've had enough of this! To hell with you, Dennis, and everybody else!" I shouted. I stormed out of the facility.

I felt devastated by the growing sense that the last five years of trying to prove myself now seemed all in vain. After working so hard, I had just thrown my air traffic control career out the window. Not only that, but my wife and kids were gone. I'd probably lost them forever.

I drove aimlessly around the city for hours. I searched desperately to find some sort of reason to explain why this was happening at this point in my life. Of course, there were no clues. I faced the realization of going home to an empty house; or so I thought.

Scene 22

INT—WILL AND LISA'S HOME—FAMILY ROOM

I arrived home that night only to find several unfamiliar cars parked in my driveway. I had to park down the street because the car owners were courteous enough to block the entrance to my own garage.

As I approached my house, the sound of music could be heard a block away, and I thought, "Someone's having a party in my house but somehow neglected to invite me."

I put the key in the lock and entered. I wasn't ready for what I discovered. I walked slowly around the room, taking in all the festivities. My family room was crowded with men and women; drinking, drugging, sexing, and doing whatever else that came to mind. I had never seen so many drugs in my life, and for that reason, I knew James had to be the ringleader.

Through the crowd, I spotted James. He was sitting in my favorite recliner, dressed in one of my suits. He was in the company of three women; two of them were seated on the floor on each sides of the recliner, the other on his lap.

James stood to greet me as I approached. "What's up, li'l brother?"

"What the hell do you think you're doing, James?"

"Heyyy…you know me. It's Friday, and you know what that means. It's on at my place."

"This is my place!"

James smiled and said, "I figured you could use some cheering up."

"Don't you realize it's because of this that my wife and kids aren't coming home?" I asked angrily as I pointed around the room.

James leaned over and whispered in my right ear, "Let Lisa run back to her Buppie parents. 'Sides, these girls said they was willin' to do thangs to make you forget all bout Lisa."

I looked James in the eye and it was at that point that I realized he was beyond saving.

Quietly, I said, "That's it. You're done. You were always the strong one, like Daddy. You could have made something out of your life, but you've never had any dreams...any ambitions."

I began to walk away and James followed, staggering with each step.

"That's it. Preach on, li'l brother," James said jokingly.

"No more preaching, James. My *Brotherly Love* just ran out!"

I picked up the telephone and dialed 911. "I need the police at..."

Before I could finish the sentence, James ripped the phone from the wall and punched me in the face.

I was momentarily stunned. Then I shoved James in the chest with the force of all the frustration inside me. Striding to my gun case, I opened it, took out my handgun, and pointed it at him.

"You ever hurt me or my family again, so help me I'll kill you where you stand!"

James ignored my warning. "You don't have the guts. 'Sides, Mama would never forgive you."

James lunged forward, grabbing hold of the gun. We both struggled desperately to gain possession. From that point on, everything seemed to happen in slow motion.

A bright flash...a deafening boom...and then James, clutching his side, falling to the floor. From what seemed like a long distance, I heard screams. The crowd in the house began scattering like ants.

I couldn't comprehend how seriously he'd been hurt. *"YOU SEE WHAT YOU MADE ME DO? GET UP, DAMN IT! GET UP!"*

Blood gushed from the wound. His white dress shirt went red. James coughed, gasping for air. I stared down at him, unable to believe what I'd done but knowing it was true. I had shot my own brother. And now there he lay, fighting for his life.

I knelt beside him. *"Damn you, James! Why you make me do that! I'm so sorry, James...Don't you die on me, damn you!"*

Although it seemed like an eternity, paramedics arrived on the scene in minutes. They wheeled James out of the house on a stretcher as several police officers escorted his party guests out in handcuffs.

Distraught, I sat on the edge of the sofa with my face buried in my hands. A detective knelt in front of me, taking notes and asking questions about the night.

"Well, it's been one helluva day for you, Mr. Taylor, but I think we got it," the detective said. "Some witnesses verified your claim of self defense, and it seems someone took the liberty of disposing of whatever drugs there might have been before we got here. We made several arrests for outstanding warrants but that's about it. However, this investigation is far from over," he said as he stood and offered his hand in sympathy.

Reluctantly, I shook the detective's hand as he and the rest of the police officers left the house.

I retrieved the telephone from the kitchen and returned to the sofa to force myself to make the call I'd been dreading. I dialed Mama's number and waited for her to answer. The answering machine kicked in on the fourth ring.

"Hi, Mama…I'm afraid I have bad news," and I continued the sad message.

I ended the phone call by saying, "I hope in time you will find a way to forgive me. Always remember that you did a wonderful job raising both of us. I'm sorry it had to end this way. I love you very much, and I always will."

I placed the telephone on the coffee table. I picked up the small picture frame containing the family portrait of Lisa, the kids, and myself. I clutched it with both hands. A thousand thoughts raced through my mind as I wondered what to do next.

Lisa and the kids pulled up in time to see the police officers and the detective leaving the house. They ran into the house, frantically searching for me, and burst into the family room.

Lisa and I embraced. "You okay?" she asked.

"No," I said.

I put my face in my hands. "My best friend betrayed me, I shot my brother, I probably lost my job and my family…GOD!"

Lisa placed my head on her shoulder, "Baby, we're gonna be all right…now what are you gonna do?"

"I don't know," I said.

Lisa grabbed me by the shoulders and firmly said, "Everything will work out!"

I looked at Lisa with the horrors of the day on my face.

I tried to regain my composure. I embraced Corey, hoping to convince him that Dad was all right.

My thoughts went back to my brother. "What about James?" I said, "Mama won't understand. I was the only chance James had."

My reference to James upset Kristin. She stood in the far corner of the family room, keeping her distance. In Kristin's eyes, James could never do any wrong. Therefore, she refused to accept the fate of her favorite uncle.

I approached Kristin with outstretched arms. However, after seeing blood on the family room carpet and hearing me confess to Lisa that I shot James, she wasn't ready to forgive me.

Frightened and confused, Kristin yelled, *"You hurt Uncle James!"* She ran out of the family room and darted up the stairs, with Lisa chasing behind.

EXT—BACKYARD OF RESIDENCE ON LAKE— INDIANAPOLIS, INDIANA—"3 YEARS LATER"— (BACK TO OPENING SCENE)

When we were kids, my mother read biblical scriptures to James and me as bedtime stories. My favorite passages were from the book of Job, in the Old Testament. Job was tested with many trials and tribulations in his life but never wavered in his faith. It was ironic that my life had come full circle. I found myself praying to God and reading that same passage in the Bible to help me get through these trying times.

As I feared, the events of that night at my home had a devastating effect on my mother. The news of James being shot was too much for her to bear. Unable to deal with the situation, my mother's health failed to the point of a stroke.

I still blame myself, as well as James, for my mother's pain. For that reason, it's been three long years and I still can't find the strength to see Mama's face again.

Occasionally, when I talk with my mother on the telephone, she often says, "Will, I understand what you did, and I forgive ya. I still love you and I always will."

I desperately want to believe her, but our conversations are quite different from what they once were. The scars run deep. Just the mention of my brother's name causes my mother to break down in tears.

Although my mother has almost fully recovered from her stroke, I know that seeing my face again might cause her more harm than good. Of course, she'll never admit it.

Surprisingly, James made sure that no charges were filed in relation to the shooting, by claiming responsibility for all the events that night. It was just another example of his strong but so often misguided character.

After recovery of his gunshot wound, he resumed his normal life of drugs, living on the street and in homeless shelters. Later that year, he was arrested in a crack house raid and convicted of drug possession. He received a sentence of several years in prison.

James often writes letters to my mother. With each letter, he asks for forgiveness of the way he treated her in the past. However, he still can't find it in his heart to forgive me. I really don't expect him to. Knowing that he has respect for my mother again helps some, though.

My battle with the air traffic facility in Louisville proved to be quite trying. Headquarters received an anonymous copy of the racist newsletter and descended upon the facility like a S.W.A.T. team at a hostage situation. Steve, the facility manager, never saw it coming.

The investigative process lasted several months. In retaliation, I found myself being verbally reprimanded by different supervisors on bogus complaints. The complaints ranged from being accused of wearing too much cologne to being accused of stealing someone's lunch from the break room refrigerator. The reprimands were all verbal, of course -- nothing in writing. No paper trail. It was just their way of retaliating.

Networking on my own, I found a facility manager who was willing to accept my transfer, and I was on my way to a new air traffic facility in Indianapolis, Indiana. Steve couldn't do anything to deny the transfer without facing the wrath of Headquarters.

Steve took one last shot at a final retaliation.

With an ear-to-ear grin, looking like a cat that had just cornered its prey, he sarcastically said, "I'm sorry, Will, we're short on manpower. I'll be delaying your departure date for three months. Also, since your move is considered a voluntary transfer; the agency can but isn't required to pay your relocation expenses. I'll be making sure they don't pay for yours!"

My last words to Steve: "God help the next African American male who comes through these doors!"

"How do you know there will be another one?" he said.

My family and I arrived in Indianapolis during the summer of 1996. The air traffic career I'd always longed for had brought me to the air traffic automation department at Indianapolis Center.

It's a small operation. Besides myself, it has five other specialists. Although I'm still the only minority, it's a very pleasant working environment; much different from Louisville.

When I first arrived, I was skeptical and didn't know what to expect. My manager quickly put my fears to rest by saying, "Will, I assure you that as long as I'm manager, nothing like what happened at your previous facility in Louisville will ever happen in my department!"

From that point on, I knew I'd made the right decision in coming to Indianapolis. Although the other automation specialists are nearly 20 years my elders, we enjoy a great rapport and kid about the age difference.

In the three years since we've come to Indianapolis, Lisa and I have managed to restore our happy family. Having a home built on a lake has been a dream come true for us. We thank God every day for our blessings.

Initially, Kristin and Corey asked about their Uncle James all the time. But as the months passed, they did so less and less. For now, the trauma of that horrid night in Louisville seemed to have very little impact.

Kristin maintained high honor-roll status during her fifth grade year and received the President's Award for her accomplishments. Now, in junior high school, she's a straight-A student and a true testament of being wise beyond her years.

Corey is an exceptional student as well and continues to be chased by girls at recess. Occasionally, he awakens in the middle of the night from a nightmare. I still open the bedroom door very slowly, cautiously checking his hands to see whether he has anything to throw at me.

We're off to Disney World for summer vacation this year.

Lisa suggested, "Why don't you call your mother and invite her to come along with us on vacation?"

I've given it some thought. This could be the perfect opportunity to put our relationship back on track.

Maybe I will! I hope and pray to God Almighty that He'll give us the strength to face each other again.

FADE OUT:

"THE END."

ABOUT THE AUTHOR

Will Sims was born and raised in the small town of Brandon, Mississippi, and is a 1981 honors graduate of Brandon High School. He is also a magna cum laude graduate of Indiana Wesleyan University, and is employed with the Federal Aviation Administration as an Air Traffic Controller.

An avid Indianapolis Colts and Indiana Pacers fan, Will currently resides in Indianapolis, Indiana, with his wife Lisa, and their two children, Kristin and Corey. His previous works consist of short stories and novels, however, *"Brotherly Love,"* is his first produced novel and screenplay.

Although Will considers writing strictly a hobby, he dreams of becoming a full time writer. He believes the major problems in society exist due to the decline of family values, and has vowed to continue writing life-affirming material.

Send questions or comments to: SmlTwnEnt@aol.com.